Musical Pulpits

Clergy and Laypersons
Face the Issue of Forced Exits

Musical Pulpits

Clergy and Laypersons
Face the Issue of Forced Exits

Rodney J. Crowell

BAKER BOOK HOUSE
Grand Rapids, Michigan 49516

ISBN: 0-8010-2568-0

Scripture quotations are taken from the New International Version of the
Bible © 1973, 1978, 1984 International Bible Society. Used by permission
of the Zondervan Bible Publishers.

The names of individuals and identifiable circumstances of personal stories
have been changed to protect privacy.

Printed in the United States of America

To my wife

Jeana

Many women do noble things,
but you surpass them all (Prov. 31:29).

Contents

Foreword

Pastoral aids and books abound to help ministers deal with the routines and crises of the ministry. Yet there are few resources to help churches and pastors deal with a problem that most will either experience or help a friend through—forced dismissal of a pastor or staff member. Few pastors-in-training or pastors-in-ministry can afford to ignore the sage advice offered here. For those pastors and churches wanting to avoid a forced exit and for those trying to heal from one, this book is required reading.

Rodney Crowell matured through the experience of a forced exit; he then studied and researched the topic. The result is this book—the most helpful and thorough available. Pastoral sensitivity, hard-earned wisdom, refreshing insights, theological analysis coupled with empirical research, and practical steps for prevention and healing set this book apart. The role of church discipline in preventing the abomination of a ruptured church is presented with scriptural faithfulness, compassion, and practical insight. Suggestions for the restoration of the nearly extinct practice of church discipline offers to the church a cure for much of the epidemic of forced pastoral exits.

As Christians we long for the eternal kingdom where strife and pain will end. Until then the wise pastor and church board will seek for wisdom "that she may guard thee."

Michael P. Green

Preface

     Forced pastoral exits are painful, embarrassing, and aggravating to all involved. Why dwell on them? Isn't it better to write about "Leadership Qualities of Successful Pastors" or "Ten Steps to Church Growth"?

     The answer is *no* and this book explains why. Previous research has established forced exits as a problem that pastors ignore at their own peril. A 1984 survey indicated that 60 percent of terminated Southern Baptist pastors were unaware that the churches that forced them out did the same to one or more of their predecessors.[1] Second, forced exits are the primary symptom of spiritual problems in congregations. As such they yield an opportunity to study their causes, dynamics, and prevention in greater detail. However, to learn from these misfortunes we must face a barrage of unpleasant facts with full confidence in a sovereign God—then boldly take corrective action.

     I doubt that I would have expended the time and money to research this issue without having experienced a forced exit myself. That story in condensed form may be found in another place.[2] This unexpected trial led me to wonder how many other pastors had had similar experiences, so I conducted a national survey of 836

Protestant pastors of whom 386 responded. The pastors were randomly selected from a church-supply magazine list of 200,000 addresses—roughly half the number of churches in the nation. Thus the sample used for this study is representative of American churches generally.

From the survey data, both verbal and quantitative, emerged some significant findings which may open up this formerly taboo subject to constructive interdenominational discussion and action.

I wish to thank all who helped me to get at the facts regarding church discipline and forced pastoral exits.

Acknowledgments

To my fantastic survey-mailing team, consisting of sons *Nathan, Peter, Gabriel,* and daughter *Rachael;*

To *Michael P. Green* of Moody Graduate School who critiqued both this manuscript and its prototype "Forced Pastoral Exit Data Analysis," while serving as my Independent Study Advisor at Dallas Theological Seminary;

To *Paul Engle* for his exemplary patience and expert assistance;

To my fellow leaders at Emmaus Church who model the godly leadership and gentle discipline described in this book's final chapter; and above all,

To the pastors and lay leaders whose survey responses broadened my horizon far beyond my own limited experience. May those who read this book consider the effort worthwhile and join us in working toward a solution.

1

Introduction to the Issue of Forced Exits

He is a gifted evangelistic pastor. Let's call him Ken. He exudes passion for souls and knows what he's about. Not surprisingly his church was growing at a fast pace. So I was astounded when he stuck his head in my doorway and said, "Let me tell you about my forced exit."

His congregation was the daughter church of a larger church in the area. One of its founding elders wanted the church to stay a "holy huddle." Upset over new people coming in, the elder began to pick at the length of Ken's preaching. Ken did his best to accommodate the demands regarding punctuality, stopping one sermon well before its end to close on time. Soon other complaints against Ken arose, centering around the vague charge of pride. Ken's elder board called in leaders from the mother church to "mediate," but by that time tensions had built to the point where Ken chose to resign.

Ken's congregation, uninformed of all this, was shocked and angry when it learned the truth—too late.

Although Ken's hard-driving leadership created unnecessary division in the congregation, this was a clear case of sabotage in a growing church—of irreversible damage done to a successful, thriving ministry in that city. Ken's story is a prime example of one of the biggest misconceptions pastors have about forced exits: "It won't happen to me if my church grows." Here are some others which inhibit corrective action:

> *"It won't happen to me if they like me."*
> Menno Epp remarked in his 1984 case study of forced exits that "congregations are easily immobilized into silence and inaction by disgruntled members. . . . "[1]
> Worse, the issues leading up to termination seldom appear in the church board's official minutes so congregations rarely have any advance warning. Your friends won't have an opportunity to defend you.

> *"Forced exits are God's way of weeding out the unfit."*
> Wrong. Studies of ex-pastors since 1932 show that it is the more talented and self-motivated ministers who leave work due to the church's ineptness and bickering.

> *"It only happens among the young and inexperienced."*
> More pastors age 35–49 endure forced exits than any other age group, and by a very wide margin. Pastors age 20–34 have the second lowest number, next to those age 65 and older.

"Forced exits help to get rid of excess clergy."
Not really. Studies by Jud (1970) and Nauss (1973)
show that only one or two percent of all pastors
leave their profession each year. Census data show
that they stay in their work 15.8 years, on average—longer than those in most other vocations.
Only barbers, farmers, and railroad conductors stay
in their vocations longer.[2]

"It only happens to the losers."
This prejudice arises from a wrong inference: the
pastor is silent about his forced exit, therefore, he
must be at fault. In recent years that has reversed:
Speed Leas discovered in his 1980 survey on forced
exits that pastors were willing to talk about their
trauma while the churches that fired them kept
mum, claiming that "reopening old wounds"
would be harmful.[3] Now that churches are silent,
why assume that the pastor is to blame?

Pastoral counselors seek to change adversaries into
teammates by encouraging them to attack the problem
rather than each other. Something similar must happen
between pastors (or church executives) and lay leaders
to break the conspiracy of silence on forced pastoral
exits.

Why Worry?

Isn't the loss of a job an occupational hazard for
everybody? Lee Iacocca was fired and rose above it. Why
can't more ministers do the same? The answer is that
we pastors can and do rise above our circumstances; yet
if a Fortune 500 corporation discovered that 30, or 50, or
even 60 percent of its managers were being forced out of
their jobs, they would identify the problem and fix it

quickly. Churches should do the same because these figures are comparable to the frequency of forced pastoral exits in some denominations! By now you have either experienced a forced pastoral exit or know someone who has.

Consequently, this problem is no longer a mere occupational hazard but a sin which must be exposed, confessed, and forsaken before it spreads to corrupt every remaining part of the body of Christ in America.

There's another good reason to worry about forced pastoral exits. In most cases they add nothing to the spiritual maturity of a pastor or church. When the pastor is fired due to his sin (or the sin of someone in the congregation), no one really learns from the experience. The pastor moves, the members stay, and whatever wrong behavior each may be guilty of goes uncorrected. The process merely begins again with a new cast of characters—a tremendous loss of an opportunity to grow in Christ.

As a result of the deplorable conduct both of pastors and church members in many forced exits, Christianity is losing credibility in America. Imagine the chagrin of a United Methodist parish whose pastor was committing adultery at the same time the Jim Bakker affair was splayed all over television screens and the front page of the *National Enquirer.* The sin of a pastor was initially a tragedy, then a standing joke. Seizing on such high-profile sins, media portrayals of clergy are to an overwhelming degree that of shady, shoddy characters.

Commenting on another fiasco, the Marian Guinn "invasion of privacy" trial in Oklahoma, Charles Colson has written:

> If we're honest, we have to admit the world's view of
> us is not so far from the mark. Our culture doesn't think

that morality is any of our business because they haven't seen us *make* it our business.

It will be bad news if the court should emasculate the church by holding that it can't enforce biblical standards on its members, but it will be even worse if it turns out that by ignoring our biblical responsibilities we have done it to ourselves.[4]

Guinn rejected her church's discipline and sued. But the point is that those who say that the church has no business "prying" into its members' lives thus find themselves in agreement with a hostile world, fraternizing with the enemy!

A Symptom of Dying Churches

Still unconvinced? Forced exits are a symptom of dying churches. Speed Leas's research revealed that church membership remained stable after a pastor's termination, but worship attendance and giving dropped off in most instances. Eventually members develop a pattern of retreating to the fringe of participation. Thus forced exits demoralize both congregations and pastors.

A Drain on Executive Energy

Denominational executives ought to be concerned about forced pastoral exits for two additional reasons. First, the task of filling constant pastoral vacancies in churches occupies far too much of their time. Second, frequently they are unable to be a "pastor to pastors" and a job placement official simultaneously. This insight is supported by Leas, who discovered that "70% of the executives thought they had a pastoral relationship with the clergy, but only 45% of the clergy thought they had pastoral relationships with the executive."[5] Edgar W. Mills surveyed 60 Presbyterian ex-pastors as part of his

1966 Ph.D. work. He suggested a possible source of friction between pastor and executive:

> Even if an executive remembers his own experience quite accurately, he tends to have been better pleased, less conflicted, more successful, more rewarded, better accepted among both lay and clergy, and more at home with the organizing tasks of the parish, than is the pastor. Executives also associated more freely with denominational leaders than did pastors and were more favorably oriented toward their views and approval. These differences may make the church executive's expectation of the parish minister's behavior somewhat unrealistic.[6]

This can lead to mutual alienation of one Christian leader from another, evidenced when one denominational official wrote a Doctor of Ministry thesis developing a workshop for "terminated" pastors without interviewing a single pastor! He gave reasons that "it had been done before" and that "pastors can't be objective" about their own trauma—yet presumed to know what they needed to hear.

The lay leader concerned about the spiritual state of churches today, pastors concerned about their emotional and financial vulnerability to critics, denominational leaders exhausted from meeting with angry search committees and pastors—all ought to be concerned about forced pastoral exits. As we shall see, it took several decades for Protestant churches to analyze and address this problem correctly.

2

A Brief History of the Problem

If forced exits were murders, then it took investigators fifty years to move from the bullet holes in the corpses to the smoking gun. While the "crime rate" increased, the investigation of forced pastoral exits crept slowly through four stages, struggling toward a prime suspect which will be identified in due time.

In Protestantism

The first phase focused attention on ex-pastors and their reasons for leaving the pastoral ministry. H. G. Duncan's 1932 survey of 111 ex-pastors revealed that about 39 percent left the ministry due to disappointment over the church's inefficient organization and administration, including "the uncertainty of tenure" and "low salary, standards, or practices."[1] Duncan did not elaborate on what the ministers meant by "low standards or practices," but it was a clue of things to come.

During the next three decades, 1932–1966, at least 29 other studies were done on clergy success and/or career

21

change.[2] Most of them fell into two categories: attempts to use personality or vocational tests as predictors of success in ministry, or studies of past or present seminarians to evaluate their training.

In this first phase of research, the function of the local church was virtually neglected. Attention was given to the "man and his mission" without study of the context in which the pastor served. In 1966 Edgar Mills shifted the focus to the church (stage two), noting that

> Some congregations are more conflict-prone and/or less responsive to pastoral leadership than other congregations [and] the degrees of proneness to conflict and unresponsiveness . . . are significant determinants of both job stability and perseverance in the ministry among ministers. . . . [3]

Bearing down on the root causes, Mills further remarked:

> [N]ext to the attractiveness of another position, the most-often mentioned reason for moving is the incidence of serious conflict between pastor and lay leaders, or between Assistant or Associate Pastor and Senior Pastor. . . . [T]he difficulties were usually compound rather than simple, the principle problems being, in order of decreasing frequency, personality (or leadership style) conflicts between the minister and some lay leaders, old guard vs. new guard struggles for control, racial integration issues, and conflicts over church mergers.[4]

Mills joined forces with Gerald Jud and Genevieve Burch in 1970 to co-author *Ex-Pastors,* a study of 276 active and 241 former pastors of the United Church of Christ. Three problem areas were exposed: (1) conflict with the congregations; (2) distortion of the pastoral role; and (3) personal problems, frequently marital.

When the ex-pastors were asked to rate 24 different reasons for leaving the pastorate, these three ranked the highest:

1. Disillusionment with the church's relevance to problems of the modern world (43.5%);
2. Opportunity to do specialized work or training (38.9%);
3. Very attractive type of work offered (32.8%).[5]

To a degree these facts reflect the "secular city" trend of the 1960s and 70s, where everything was branded religious: 61.5 percent of the 231 ex-pastors said they were "still in the ministry but out of the pastorate," even though most held nonchurch jobs. Only 58 percent of them said that while in seminary they were "already clear about a vocation and seeking to prepare for it." Clearly, a local church was a frustrating place for a young reformer or seeker to land—but that may have been due to the seminarian's unrealistic expectations of the church as much as any resistance from the laity.

During the 1980s, the third phase in research shifted the emphasis from ex-pastors to stressed pastors—from results to causes. *Burnout* became a buzzword. Harold Myra surveyed 500 pastors in 1981. Sixty percent of them said they had experienced a stressful event in their professional life that was difficult for them to accept. Eighty percent of these traumatized pastors admitted they had never anticipated that anything like it could happen in the ministry.[6] Charles Rassieur in 1982 authored his book, *Stress Management for Ministers,* which challenged clergy to take responsibility for their own mental health.[7]

In this era, more attention was paid to how the pastor could minimize the effect of stress on himself physically. Helpful suggestions abounded: find a fresh approach to prayer and Bible study; take time off from your work; establish a support group; exercise regularly; laugh more; enrich your family life—and so on. Congregations were told to encourage their pastor's continuing education, recognize his humanity, form more realistic expectations of the pastor's role and of his personal ministry gifts, and protect his privacy. These aided thousands of pastors, no doubt—yet forced exits continued unabated.

Getting Down to Facts

Truly empirical research of forced exits (phase four) also emerged in the 1980s as case studies and survey methods came into popularity in practical theology. The decade opened with two important studies. The first, by Tommy D. Bledsoe, found varying degrees of stress in thirteen Georgia Baptist ministerial families whose fathers had resigned under duress. Bledsoe found that in most cases, the pastor's family "pulled together" to withstand the strain, which affected the pastors much like a divorce.[8]

Speed B. Leas authored the first descriptive survey of forced exits in 1980, which remains a landmark work. He collected 117 reports of forced terminations of pastors from officials in the Presbyterian (PCUSA), Episcopal, and United Church of Christ denominations. Leas had originally planned to interview both terminated pastors and their former congregations, but 83 percent of the congregations refused to participate; hence his team opted for telephone interviews of denominational officials from districts where forced exits had transpired.[9]

The enduring value of Leas's study resides in the combination of data gathering with comparisons between the denominations. Leas was determined to discover the frequency of forced exits; the average tenure of pastors; the frequency of the main causes of forced exits; the effect of forced exits on the congregation; the amount of time the denominational executive spent with the church and terminated pastor; and the financial "settlement" of this ecclesiastical divorce.

Leas did not attempt to study associate or assistant pastors who were forcibly terminated, nor those who left their churches for reasons of "moral turpitude." Here's a sample of what he found:

> In the 3 denominations studied, 34 to 45% of the churches where forced exits happened harbored existing conflicts among members *before* the terminated pastor had begun his ministry; further, 23% of these congregations had fired or forced out previous ministers.

> Congregational stress was identified by the denominational executives as a major factor which was involved in 45% of the church battles. Value or belief conflicts were involved 28% of the time, mostly over fundamental versus liberal or charismatic versus non-charismatic theologies. Two diametrically opposed pastoral factors were tied for third place—poor leadership and authoritarian leadership.

> He also found that two-thirds of all forced exits happened within the first five years of the pastor's tenure; that the rate of forced exits was 1 in every 100 churches (underestimated perhaps because the executives, not the pastors, were surveyed); and that 38 percent of the lay leaders went to the denominational executive intent upon firing the pastor.

> The executives told Leas that they had spent an average of 35–40 hours with each termination situation, and that most pastors were given immediate severance with 90 days of pay or more.[10]

From his analysis of the data, Leas remarked that too many denominational officials and analysts seemed predisposed to blame the minister rather than look at dynamics within the congregation. Also denominational help seemed to come too late, after the die was cast for the pastor's resignation.

In 1984 Menno H. Epp authored *The Pastor's Exit;* it contained his interviews of thirty-five Canadian Mennonite pastors who had been terminated, representing one-fifth of all Mennonite Conference Canadian churches. Epp was also able to interview "numerous" representatives of congregations that had forcibly terminated pastors. His description of the dynamics of forced exits includes the use of the high percentage required in a confidence vote (usually from 66 to 90 percent) to force out an undesired pastor.

Other dynamics of forced exits include the destruction of the pastor's self-image through criticism; hurt and withdrawal by the pastor's spouse and family; lack of close friends due to vulnerability; expectations for the pastor to be good at everything he does; and the weakened trust in new pastors created by unresolved conflicts in previous forced terminations.[11]

Epp's recommendations for the Canadian Mennonite churches were that the pastors accept and move toward a partnership ministry with the laity; that pastors be given the right to appeal a nonconfidence vote; and that each congregation have a pastor-church relations committee with a clear review process. He further recommended that pastors should be granted tenure after six years of satisfactory ministry; and that congregations be accountable to lay-clergy review committees from other regions who would require congregation leaders to give a regular verbal report on the state of the church.

Mennonite leaders replied that implementation of these recommendations would need to proceed slowly and cautiously. One important note for Mennonites, who have traditionally placed great emphasis on fraternal admonition and correction in the local church: Epp says that at no time was Christ's rule of discipline (Matt. 18:15–17) ever used to facilitate discussion between the pastor and the church. While this is a tragedy among all churches, for Mennonites it suggests a serious neglect of this historic strength.

The largest survey on pastoral terminations to date was released in June of 1984. It was conducted by Cliff Tharp of the Research Services Department of the Southern Baptist Convention.[12] Names of ministers forcibly terminated were secured through denominational channels and four hundred cases were systematically studied.

The two most frequently stated reasons for forced pastoral exits were "a small but powerful minority of members" (66 percent of the situations reporting this) and "factions in the congregation" (41 percent). Obviously, both factors may be present simultaneously.

Half of the ministers responding to the survey had been forced out within three years or less of their arrival, and 78 percent of the churches had terminated previous pastors, a rate much higher than that reported in the 1980 Alban Institute study. Fifty-nine percent of the pastors said they were unaware of the church's history of forced terminations when they came.

The Research Services Department estimated from the available data that, in a year's time, 1,056 Southern Baptist pastors suffer forced exits. A 1988 study revised that estimate upward to 1200 pastors annually. (Ernest White's 1989 study of the Missouri Southern Baptist Convention concluded that if Missouri's rate is characteristic of the SBC nationally, then the rate of forced exits nationwide would only be half of the two previous projections averaged together, or 564 pastors each year.)[13]

In 1986 Tharp's colleague Brooks Faulkner published his book *Forced Termination,* incorporating findings from workshops he conducted with terminated pastors in eight states. Faulkner advocates "retraining" workshops for pastors and churches in which deacon boards and pastors clarify their concepts of biblical beliefs, mission, and spiritual growth.[14] Surely this is preferable to uncontrolled confrontation; yet given the high number (78 percent) of churches with at least one forced termination in the Southern Baptist Convention, retraining seems an overwhelming task.

Faulkner divided the reasons for forced exits into two main categories: "Why Ministers Become Expendable" and "Why Churches Become Dissatisfied with Ministers." Obviously there can be overlap between the two. Reasons for forced exits falling into the former category include: rigidity (pastor's inability to change); tenure; "subterranean pastors" (Faulkner's euphemism for contentious members); "deaconphobia"; loss of respect or trust; and incompetence (either in personal or interpersonal skills).[15]

In the latter category are: stress within congregations; neighboring churches' growing; spiritual stagnation; "fire the coach" mentality; pastors not getting along with key persons; or having offensive manners or appearance. A pastor can be fired for just about anything. But who is to decide whether he will be fired? That decision, it appears, results from years of interpersonal strife which prods pastors into giving up. Jewish researchers see much the same pressures on Conservative and Reform rabbis, making this a truly ecumenical problem.

On Monday the Rabbi Resigned

Studies on rabbinical stress and ex-rabbis first appeared in the 1980s as two Jewish scholars broke existing taboos of silence on these subjects. Rabbi Richard Schachet gathered for a two-day workshop six men who had left the full-time rabbinate. Most of them had formed informal groups *(havuroth)* meeting less frequently for worship and discussion. They supplemented their income by performing weddings and other life-cycle services.

Schachet found that much of the workshop participants' frustration in the full-time rabbinate involved their work with people in their congregations who were minimally Jewish and who saw the rabbi as one through whom they could vicariously be Jewish. (Schachet himself mentions that he once served a Conservative congregation which expected him to keep a strict kosher diet although they themselves did not.)[16] The ex-rabbis felt the *havuroth* supply a more purposeful Jewish-based religious community for themselves and their fellow members, yet at the cost of a full-time salary—and, Schachet says, at the expense of organized Judaism, which needs an internal force for reformation.

Rabbi Leslie Freedman's 1982 survey of 1,342 Conservative and Reform rabbis helped to reveal other problems. Several factors contributing to the rabbis' psychological distress in his study were: failure of the rabbi to distinguish sufficiently between his role and his personal life; the attitude of his wife toward the rabbinate; lowered self-esteem from an inability to meet his own expectations of moral perfection; and what Freedman calls "generalized expressions of job dissatisfaction," involving such matters as career advancement potential and salary level.[17]

Yet it is the degree of role-related stress in his study that I find most surprising. Freedman discovered that the average rabbi has a level of stress greater than 63 percent of the general population in the United States. In fact when compared to the stress level of the adult male population in the vicinity of the Three Mile Island nuclear reactor in the month following the infamous accident there, the rabbis' stress level is higher—and, quite obviously—sustained for a longer period of time.[18]

We may provisionally conclude that rabbinical stress stems from two major sources: conflict between the rabbi and the nominally Jewish members of his congregation (which could include even those in lay leadership positions), and the inner conflicts of the rabbi. These concern (but are certainly not limited to) his own expectations for setting an impeccable moral example, while balancing the demands of his public and private life. Evidently these conflicts intensify when the rabbi occupies a full-time, salaried position as spiritual leader of a congregation.

Protestant clergy may easily recognize problems in the rabbinate which run parallel to their own struggles. If powerful individuals or warring groups in the local church or synagogue are exerting powerful judgmental influence over their paid leaders, deciding the issue of their competence in the absence of any other spiritual authority, that situation will of necessity create the agonizing event of a forced exit. The next two chapters will tell you what that is like (if you don't already know!).

3

Warning Signals

A pastor alert to warning signs of a forced exit may be able to negotiate a new agreement for future ministry (or at least an orderly and fair departure), before increasing pressure tempts him to make too many concessions. That's the reason for this chapter—but first, a personal story:

It was a big, beige-brick battleship of a church, replete with stained glass, bell tower, and huge educational wing. Its four-hundred-plus members were your typically decent suburbanites—active in the community, talented, with many corporate-type people. And I was their new pastor!

The search committee said they wanted spiritual renewal and I considered my unanimous election a mandate to pursue that goal. But we had misunderstood each other: "spiritual renewal" for them meant they wanted a big wheel in the community like their beloved former pastor. I thought they wanted to put Jesus Christ first in their lives, turn back to the Bible, and become evangelistic.

I had heard some rumblings about how the previous pastor "burned out" in his job and left to teach in the public schools. I had also heard that one lady ran the church with her money, but she seemed so personable, humble, and hardworking that I dismissed that idea.

Then the warning signals began but I didn't recognize them. One of our deacons resigned from the board for flimsy reasons. The youth group began to fall apart when school started. The widow of a beloved former pastor and her family stopped attending. Then, as a result of a city ministerium meeting, I authored a statement calling on the churches, schools, and homes to work together in reducing the pressures on the family. It appeared in the local newspaper. The Band and Drill Team Boosters didn't like it because many felt it was more exciting to be competing in football stadiums than to be in church on Sunday. A few more empty spaces began to appear in the pews.

As I sensed more defections due to lack of commitment, I began to "preach heavy" on repentance and discipleship.

I began giving invitations to receive Jesus Christ as Savior. One young man shocked everyone by actually responding and walking down the aisle! Sermon outlines with Scripture references began to appear regularly in the bulletin. And some people began bringing their Bibles to worship, not just to Sunday school.

The first complaint had to do with the Bibles. Some members felt that it was distracting to hear the pages rustling as others followed me through the Word. (They didn't have that problem with the hymnbook, I noted.) Then they said my sermons were too long—ten to fifteen minutes past the appointed hour. Then they began picking at our associate pastor, putting pressure on me to fire her. I refused, being convinced that the problem was our lack of commitment, not her lack of leadership.

Then came a drop in giving. Our treasurer said we were having to borrow from our Capital Fund account to meet payroll. He gave no explanation. Were just a few families withholding their contributions intentionally, or was the whole church fed up with me?

An "inflexible" stage came next. Tensions grew, and the wise man of the congregation told me that I should tone down my preaching. On my birthday I was told by our elders that I was doing a lousy job and had everybody upset because I was "acting like a Baptist preacher." I didn't think that was so bad but they did.

I announced my resignation from the pulpit one Sunday. The deacon who had resigned (the first warning signal, remember?) grinned broadly at me. I had lasted three-and-a-half years. In the last seven months before moving away, our family experienced a mixture of gracious gestures and dirty little tricks. Our opponents would leave nasty messages on the answering machine and drive past our home in surveillance. An elder who had praised my ministry a year ago now passed me on the street without a greeting or eye contact. Our friends gave us deeply touching notes and letters, money from their tax refund, and a counted cross-stitch of Matthew 18:19–20 which I cherish. They were like Elijah's ravens to me.

Had I or my lay leaders noted the warning signals and confronted the problem head-on, I might have resigned under more friendly circumstances. Then again, if that had happened, I probably wouldn't know what I know now.

Research by Speed Leas in 1980 and Cliff Tharp in 1984 mentioned earlier shows that half of all forced pastoral exits are preceded by warning signs similar to those in my own case.

Frequent complaints
Withdrawal from pastor and church
Drop in attendance or financial giving
Sudden changes in lay leadership
Inflexibility by pastor and/or people

Still about 44 percent of all forced exits take place
suddenly—but that's not the problem. The problem is
that many pastors resign before the appropriate body—
the congregation—has the opportunity to discuss and
decide on the matter. That's what I did, and now I ask
myself why I didn't call for a congregational meeting.

As part of its political maneuvering or intimidation,
an unofficial church kingpin or leadership board may
seek to force the pastor's resignation through several
lines of argument. I chart some from Howard Pendley,
coupled with suggested pastoral countermoves presented in condensed form.[1] (I add my own suggestions
in parentheses.)

Reasons Given Why You Should Resign	**Responses Which You Should Consider**
"Many members are un-happy with your ministry"	Who? How many? Call for a vote.
"Many have said they won't attend or give as long as you're the pastor."	What do the financial records show? Can the church still function? (Ask for an audit.)
"Our church is polarized; unless you leave soon, we'll have a hopelessly divided congregation."	Has this happened before? Then the pastor may not be the problem. (Ask for an impartial mediator.)

"If you force a vote, there will be a terrible church fight and the church will split."

Church splits aren't that likely. (Ask the members if the church board has kept them informed.)

"Why put your family through such trauma as a fight?"

Moving is traumatic, too. Tell your board this, and weigh your options.

"We'll give you a chance to find a new job. Your next church won't have to know about all this trouble."

"There is nothing hid that shall not come to light." Refuse to be a co-conspirator.

"How can you expect to pastor effectively, knowing so many don't want you to stay?"

Same as above: How many is many? Get a vote.

In some cases, the pastor must learn to stand his ground against vocal minorities, but what are his alternatives if he does so?

Both the pastor and the church board must cooperate in order to forge alternatives to forced exits. The church board must do its part by distinguishing between legitimate and illegitimate reasons for firing a pastor. Legitimate reasons would include *violations of scriptural injunctions; sexual offenses* (rape, adultery, incest, sodomy, homosexuality [Lev. 20:10–18]); *violent crimes* (murder or kidnapping [Exod. 21:12–17]); *gossip* (Prov. 20:19); or *lying* (Col. 3:9); as well as *greed, slander, drunkenness, or swindling* (1 Cor. 5:9–11). *Failure to keep confidence* (Prov. 18:7) *or to have a servant attitude* (1 Peter 5:3) would also provide just cause for termination—if these sins went uncorrected after repeated warnings. To prevent a frame-up, two eyewitnesses are required (see 1 Tim. 5:19). However, a pastor should *not* be fired merely because he has "locked horns" with a wealthy or influential board member. Similarly a pastor should not be forced out if there has been numerical or spiritual growth, or if he demonstrates willingness to repent and grow through receiving admonition and correction.

What must the pastor do to fulfill his duty when pressure to resign builds? Above all he should place the church's interests ahead of his own when evaluating the matter of staying or leaving. Needless to say consideration such as his children's schooling, his reputation or income, or his desire to be vindicated do not keep the church's welfare in mind. The pastor can show good faith by refusing to attack critics from the pulpit and by agreeing to meet with the critics if they welcome the opportunity.

Given these basic ground rules, what alternatives to resignation exist? Brooks Faulkner lists five:

1. Using an outside mediator—a denominational executive or a mutually respected pastor in the case of independent churches
2. Establish goals for reinstatement of the pastor after receiving counseling or training for his personal problems or deficiencies
3. Giving the minister the right to attend all meetings where charges are levied against him
4. Repentance on the part of both pastor and people
5. A leave of absence by the pastor to get perspective[2]

As mentioned earlier Faulkner advocates retraining seminars to allow pastors and deacon boards to renegotiate their ministry.[3] This is fine—if the deacons are willing. If they get enough pressure from their fellow members, they may not be. Yet anything which will prevent both sides from a hasty, ill-considered resignation is to be taken seriously.

Congregations need to realize that a successfully endured crisis is one way in which a pastor becomes established in a church—and that once a pastor has proved his intent to stay with a congregation through thick and thin, then the most fruitful years of his ministry often lie just ahead. Sadly it is just beginning to dawn on some observers of Christianity that many churches are unwilling to let any pastor reach that point of fruitfulness.

4

The Emotional Toll
of Forced Exits

A forced exit represents a potent attack on a pastor at his most vulnerable moment. Blaming others won't help alleviate the pain, for no one gets through a forced exit smelling like a rose. The experience of ecclesiastical divorce aggravates the tendency of our sinful nature toward anger, anxiety, depression, self-pity, and vengeance.

The emotional toll of forced exits may be reduced by anticipating what effect they will have on the pastor, and by knowing how to survive them. The first is the subject of this chapter; the second will be discussed in the next chapter.

Russell Cawthon, Jr., aptly summarizes what a pastor loses in a forced exit as social life, salary, and self-esteem.[1] He loses all three together, and quickly.

Loss of Social Life

The loss of social life reminds a pastor of how much his personal life is dominated by church relationships.

Once he has been forced to resign, it is hard to maintain them. Many people in the congregation are attached to him because of his position, not his personality. When his job ends, his relationship with them ends, although Christmas cards help prolong the communication a bit.

Then there are his true friends. It's hard to associate with them after a resignation because the mutual pain dominates the conversation—its words and its silences. Every phone call, every visit has a note of finality.

His family feels the disruption as well. They have friends in the congregation too. Young children can't comprehend why Daddy isn't wanted anymore. But who can *they* talk to? They can't afford a counselor now, so pastoral families turn to each other through simple daily pleasures like talking, hiking, or evening devotions that rebuild courage and faith.

If a pastor has a layover time between his last Sunday in the old church and his first Sunday in a new one, it is wise for him to swallow his pride and go to a loving, lively church fellowship nearby—one that has plenty of activities for his family that will fill in the relationship gap created by his forced exit.

Loss of Salary

Then there's salary. Most pastors don't have much to begin with, so a forced exit sets the clock ticking: How long can we go without a new church before the money runs out? When I resigned under pressure, we had two thousand dollars in the bank and received one month's severance pay. The Lord and my wife graciously stretched those dollars to last seven months until we relocated. We arrived in Kansas with all bills paid and two hundred dollars left.

Yet others have a hard time financially. Research by Leas, Tharp, and Faulkner tells us that churches are usually not very generous with terminated pastors—ninety days' severance pay is the norm.

What about emergency pay for ministers? Doesn't the denomination help them out? Only about one-third of the pastors receive such help, according to Leas, and it amounts to less than a thousand dollars in most cases— for real emergencies only. Tharp's 1984 survey of Southern Baptists shows that 50 percent of the terminated pastors had to rely on their spouses' income to help them through the "layoff period."

Looking for a temporary job isn't easy when the ex-pastor can't promise the employer that he'll stay on. It's a sin to lie about the situation, and if he's like most clergy, he lacks much experience in other lines of work.

Added to that are the hidden costs of relocation. Even if his new church pays the moving expenses, he will stand much of the cost of selling his home or unwanted furnishings (usually at a loss) and buying new. For pastoral families those expenses add up very quickly.

Unlike fired executives, most ministers don't benefit from a forced exit. Leas's survey shows that 82 percent of terminated pastors went to new churches whose salary was equal to or less than their old church.[2] When additional expenses are considered, such as paying for your own health insurance in case of a long transition, a forced exit adds up to financial loss for the pastor.

Consequently the pastor who can negotiate his departure conditions may need to insist on a more equitable settlement which includes:

1. At least four to six months' salary;
2. The continuation of health and life insurance for at least six months after the effective resignation date;
3. A stipend for transition costs which the new church won't assume: printing and postage costs

for mailing résumés or reimbursement for long-distance calls.

The terminating church won't like bargaining, but if they are willing to pay the other costs of termination, then the rest should follow.

Loss of Self-Esteem

This is the greatest test during a forced exit. It begins with that hidden message the pastor gets from the church leaders: "We have the money. We pay you. Therefore, we have the right to say it's your fault." It's very difficult to avoid resentment when he senses that kind of manipulation.

His competence and even his call to the ministry will be questioned, so he must be ready. Ira Survivor (a pseudonym) writes, "Don't consider leaving the ministry. . . . If you received God's call to the ministry and didn't quit during the good times, don't leave now. God will see you through."[3] Soon after I resigned, I received a bibliography on career change from the man who was the interim pastor at the church before I came. I took it lightly, knowing he was a friend of one of my detractors.

Add to these whatever difficulties in placement may be experienced, the denial of closure (the warm, collective congregational farewell that marks the end of a "job well done"), and the withdrawal of fellow ministers (who feel threatened by the fact that the same thing could easily happen to them), and you get a pretty potent attack on a pastor's self-esteem.

What Churches Suffer

Forced exits aren't easy on churches either. I asked eleven pastors who were professional contacts or survey respondents to provide names of sixteen lay leaders of churches that have experienced forced pastoral exits. Nine laypeople returned a one-page interview form (see *appendix B*) giving their reflections on the failures leading to forced exits, their trauma, and the lessons to be learned. Three of the lay leaders came from churches in the Southern Baptist Convention with one each from the Presbyterian, United Church of Christ, Bible Church, American Baptist, and Missionary denominations. One church was unidentified.

As to the nature of the conflict, four lay leaders indicated their former pastors were unresponsive to lay leadership or tried to monopolize the church. One felt that was justified due to an improper "power base" in the congregation. One lay leader felt her pastor lacked leadership; another said the pastor got angry at board meetings; and a third said the pastor had poor personal-spending habits. Two respondents said the pastor had done nothing wrong.

Significantly five of them said their churches had failed to apply biblical discipline. Four admitted church problems persisting to this day, including family tensions, spiritual coldness, a poor testimony in the community, loss of members, and their own social exclusion. The most drastic forced exit "fallout" was described by a laywoman from a Missionary church:

> The conflict resulted in the pastor being forced to leave. Because of this decision, the people who supported the pastor left the church. The church attendance was reduced to half, relationships were severed, weekly income was drastically cut, various ministries in the church were forced to disband, the church became known in the community as a place of power struggles, fighting, and discontent. I could go on and on!

She adds, "All my relationships have changed. Those who were opposed to the forced exit have become my closest friends. It's almost as though we went through a war together—the bonds are *strong.*"

One respondent said the church board had misused the disciplinary process, while another reported that a small power group in the church had abused it. No pastors were reported as misusing the disciplinary process in a punitive manner.

When asked, "What counsel would you offer other lay leaders to prevent or to better handle conflicts like these?" three revealing answers emerged: "Better pastoral accountability to the board" was one. Another leader replied, "The pastor should have hung on longer. His resignation short-circuited the resolution process." A third told me, "Leaders need diligently to apply biblical principles in the church. We need to address problems when they're small and involve only those directly affected." He added, "Things got pretty big before we even thought of dealing with them." By then, of course, it was too late.

This informal survey is far too small to be conclusive, yet it reveals a tendency for forced exits to harm the lives of churches as well as pastors. In describing its chilling effect on the zeal of his congregation, one lay leader said of his fellow members, "They once were 'hot' —now are not." That's a rather terse commentary on the idea that firing the pastor solves a church's problems.

Yet God in his infinite grace gives strength, wisdom, and perseverance for these trying circumstances. How can pastors and churches steer a straight course through such an emotionally charged time? The next chapter offers some survival tactics used by those who have weathered these storms.

5

Survival Steps for Pastors and Churches

To keep a forced exit from ruining the life of a pastor or a church, follow these steps for survival. Once grasped they make as much sense as heading for high ground in a flood. Pastors need to focus on emotional, spiritual, and financial survival while churches must tiptoe through forced termination using fair procedures.

For Pastors

Robert Dale uses four words to summarize the key tasks of the pastor during the trauma of forced termination: *survive, heal, grow,* and *risk.* He explains:

> *Surviving* places the energy focus on the past's losses and hurts. *Healing* shifts to the present's responsibilities. *Growing* stays with the present but puts more emphasis upon hopefulness and initiative. *Risking* directs energy on the future's plans and options.[1]

The steps of emotional and spiritual survival enable the pastor to prevent the pain of his recent rejection from influencing his present prospects for a new pulpit and a fresh start. Start at the bottom and work up through this diagram to get an overview:

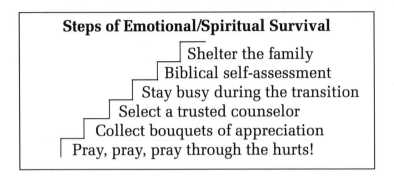

Steps of Emotional/Spiritual Survival

Shelter the family
Biblical self-assessment
Stay busy during the transition
Select a trusted counselor
Collect bouquets of appreciation
Pray, pray, pray through the hurts!

Prayer

This is where the terminated pastor will win or lose the spiritual battles of a forced exit. Here's why: a pastor will be tempted to place all the blame either on the church or on himself. Prayer draws his attention Godward to the fact that "all have sinned," and helps him begin to distinguish what people do to each other from what God does for us in redeeming love. Further, prayer for his enemies sets them beside himself as fragile, errant, fellow sinners also in desperate need of God's grace. It defuses the pastor's anger and thwarts Satan's manipulative attempts. For the next few pages, I will specifically address pastors going through the trauma of church fights and forced exits.

Don't neglect your own prayer needs. Cleanse your heart of bitterness and self-righteous anger through confession of sin; cast your cares on God in petition; remind yourself of the hope of your calling and the incomparably great power of God at work in you. Read Ephesians 1:18–19 and personalize it as you pray.

Bouquets

Now move up a step. *Start collecting bouquets*, if you haven't done so yet. Bouquets are treasured reminders of what you've done right. Notes or letters of appreciation, greeting cards for birthdays or Easter or Christmas, drawings from your children—these are visual reminders that "he who began a good work in you will carry it on to completion until the day of Christ Jesus" (Phil. 1:6a). I keep mine in what I call a "blessing file." (Other pastors call theirs a "blue Monday" file. Just be sure you have one.) One of my bouquets is a surprise note I found scribbled on the back of a list of offertory verses I used in worship on my last Sunday in "the" church. The man (who was liturgist) wrote in huge letters, underlined: THANKS FOR TOUCHING OUR LIVES.

Counselor

Step up again: *Find a trusted counselor* who can give you a listening ear and sound counsel from the Word of God. He does not have to be a close personal friend; in fact it may help if he isn't. I leaned on a fellow pastor who grew up in the church that forced me out. His understanding of people on both sides of the conflict was invaluable. He helped me discern between accurate criticism and unfair blame, while affirming my ministry.

Stay Busy

Keep climbing higher by forming an activity plan to help you resist idleness and despair. Start a new project whether it is work related or not. During my termination "layoff," I began study notes on the Book of Genesis and a year later was using them for Wednesday-

night teaching in a new church. Fill those spare
moments with purposeful activity. *Stay busy during the
transition!*

Self-assessment

Now enlist the help of your trusted friend as you
*assess your growth and the direction of your ministry
in the light of Scripture.* With his aid, study texts like
1 Peter 2:21–25 and Romans 12:14–21. Do personal
inventory. Have you confessed every sin you can recall?
Are you sure? Use your friend to evaluate your spiritual gifts and the direction of your ministry—what you
have learned over the years about pastoring, yourself,
your strengths, and weaknesses. A helpful exercise is
Ralph Neighbor's "Spiritual Gifts Inventory," available
from The Ralph Neighbor Evangelistic Association
(P. O. Box 19888, Houston, TX 77224; 713–497–7901).
This will help you find a new church that compensates
for some of your weaknesses.

Shelter the Family

Finally—and this step results from having taken all
the others—*shelter your family from as much of the
trauma of termination as you can.* Roy Price says, "Give
your children the facts [about your forced exit], but
spare them from your hostility." Make mealtime praise-
time, not gripetime, by singing and sharing the day's
blessings—what God provided or what you appreciate
about each other. I'm not fond of the shallow theology in
the Johnny Appleseed grace:

> Oh, the Lord is good to me,
> And so I thank the Lord. . . .

. . . but I do have warm memories of us singing that
around the umpteenth dinner of rice casserole during

our "exile," fully convinced in my heart that the Lord would provide for us when our future was totally uncertain. Cherish your family relationships rather than abuse them in your anger.

Two parenthetical remarks before we move on to the financial aspect. Some pastors have had to deal with "flashbacks," or hurtful incidents from the past which pop intrusively back into memory with their attendant feelings of ill will. Don't let them attack you; instead, pray for forgiveness (for yourself and your enemies), and praise God for the redemption you both have in Christ. The flashbacks may continue for two or three years, but they diminish in intensity and eventually vanish. I personally guarantee that they will! Second, show kindness to your former church. Precisely now, when you have nothing to gain vocationally from it, is the time to let your light shine. Avoid punitive behavior and do your job with integrity until the moment you hand over the keys. If you have lived in a parsonage, leave it in top shape when you move. You may not be thanked, but you'll be obedient. Which matters most to you?

Finances

How can the pastor manage finances when he no longer earns a regular paycheck? Here are some tips for financial survival:

1. Cut expenses and supplement your pay
2. Manage assets well
3. Start early on the employment search
4. Avoid welfare if possible

You can always find new ways to save money by reducing nonessential expenses. Use coupons on the supermarket weekly specials to trim food prices, cancel

cable TV or newspaper subscriptions, buy used cloth-
ing, accept hand-me-downs, lower the thermostat, repair
the old rather than replace it—the list goes on. Second,
*supplement severance pay with your spouse's or chil-
dren's income or a part-time job that leaves you free to
candidate.* I worked for a ServiceMaster franchisee cleaning a smoke-damaged apartment; it was a short-term job
that enabled me to pursue a call to another church.

Take stock of your assets, property as well as capital.
Hold garage sales to weed out what you don't need and
don't want to move. Sell the second car if you have one.
Check to see if it's worth losing the interest to cash in a
certificate of deposit or to borrow against your life insurance. Be like the steward who cut his master's losses
(Luke 16:1–13), yet remember that you can't serve God
and mammon.

*The best financial help you can give yourself is to
start early in your search for a new church.* An updated
profile or résumé should be sent out promptly. If you
are changing denominations, allow time to present your
credentials, pass examinations, and be approved to candidate in the new fellowship. When you're unemployed,
time is money! Cast your net wide by using other search
agencies as well as denominational ones. Here are three
I recommend:

> Intercristo, 19303 Fremont Ave. N., Seattle, WA
> 98133; 800–426–1342
>
> Bridge Associates, Box 1116, Winsted, CT 06098;
> 203–379–1396
>
> The Moody Referral Listing, Moody Bible Institute,
> 820 North LaSalle Dr., Chicago, IL 60610;
> 312–329–4414 (Any church but only Moody grad-
> uate pastors may use this service.)

These organizations are legitimate, highly professional services that aid denominational placement officials by relieving a small part of their workload. They also aid denominational churches by providing more pastoral candidates for them. My own experience with independent placement was a very positive one.

Unemployment Compensation

When all else fails, and you haven't yet found a church, swallow your pride and apply for unemployment compensation. If you have trouble reconciling this with 2 Thessalonians 3:10 ("If a man will not work, he shall not eat"), do public volunteer work at a worthy agency to repay your fellow taxpayers. Clifford Tharp's research indicates that only 5 percent of Southern Baptist terminated pastors had to resort to government support to feed their families. Considering a pastor's low salary, that's commendable.

Counseling

Perhaps you have seriously questioned whether or not you belong in the ministry and have raised such questions in the good times as well as the bad. If so, be honest with yourself and seek vocational counseling. It's inexpensive and readily available. Tell yourself, "I gave it my best shot and learned from it. The Lord still has need of me. I'll follow him to a new field of endeavor, singing his praises."

While the pastor moves on, members of his former church must recover and retain unity. How is this done?

For the Church

The church's survival steps are *political* in nature, using good judgment and fair procedures to effect a pastoral transition with the least disturbance and harm.

Here are some suggestions culled from the literature on forced exits:

1. *When the impasse has become absolutely hopeless, give the minister a chance to resign.*
   When is it hopeless? When the church fight has become an embarrassment in the community or when the pastor turns vindictive from the pulpit. Those are two vivid signs; an earlier one may be consistently bad board meetings.

2. *If the minister refuses to resign, announce a duly called congregational meeting to vote.*
   The vote should be taken by secret ballot, allowing the members to "save face." While many ministers would disagree, it is probable that any pastoral demand for a show of hands would be outvoted anyway. If your church constitution has a clear voting procedure, follow it without any political maneuvering.

3. *Be fair with the severance package.*
   Ninety days' salary and benefits is a "minimum for decency." Attempts to punish the minister's family could backfire. They nearly did for my former church. A few weeks after my resignation, the church board told me they wanted us out of the parsonage in two weeks, new church or not. When our friends in the church learned of this, they came to the next board meeting and sat in a ring around the room. The church board retreated in a hurry.
   It usually takes a minimum of four to six months for a minister to relocate. Understanding will smooth the change.

4. *Obtain an interim pastor quickly.*
   Executives are fired on Friday morning, and are expected to leave by day's end. Pastors can't usu-

ally do that, but they should not be expected to waddle along as lame ducks. Said one pastor in Menno Epp's interviews, "I could have cheerfully strangled them for having asked me to stay on as interim pastor until they found another."[2]

5. *Shift the leadership load away from the high-profile people or groups who fought for the pastor's removal.*

This is a smart planning move, not simply a means of smoothing over congregational differences. Speed Leas warns that a congregation can get stuck in "defensive retreat" following conflict, which is a system of control designed to insulate the organization against all change. Decision making becomes highly centralized, communication flow is greatly restricted, unconditional loyalty is expected from all people, and planning is sacrificed for expediency. Don't let it happen. Shift a few responsibilities to new people. It's also a way to make certain that the church board or search committee is truly representative of the congregation at large. If that's not true of their board now, they're asking for trouble.

When a pastor is terminated, people need to know that they are all equally important to the church. They've seen the "big wheels" wield their influence during the termination fight; now they need to be heard also.

6. *Identify your church problems and work on them.*

Are there problems with group rivalry, contentious members, lack of a clear mission, political battles with the denomination, or immorality? Get ready to fire the next pastor you hire unless you work on these problems, for he'll probably point them out to you if he's worth his salary. Confront, not deny, these problems *or they will do you in.* Never forget that bossy people will try to run you as well as the minister. Am I talking about disciplining dear old Aunt Harriet who taught Sunday school for fifty years, or Uncle Fred who donated the money for the new organ? Absolutely!

7. *When you're ready, begin searching for a new pastor.*
   If you're in a denominational church, a phone call to the appropriate authority is usually all you need to start the process rolling. In an independent church, you have to choose your channels of searching for candidates. What was said earlier to pastors applies to churches: Cast your net out wide. Then work hard on your church's self-profile to give the prospective candidate as clear an idea of your congregation as possible. Don't fudge on your church's problems but describe them simply and realistically. Some search channels require only a brief descriptive paragraph, which includes your location, size of membership, characteristics of your people, and salary package. Then be prepared for many meetings to read pastors' profiles, discuss, vote, and do interviews. In the long run, you're far better off keeping a good minister if you have one because this is hard work.

8. *Re-establish respect for ministry generally.*
   Forced terminations accompanied with great animosity toward a particular minister tend to breed a rebellious attitude toward authority generally. As spiritual leaders in your congregation, that's a

setup for rebellion against *you* if you don't control it. One way is discipline; another way is to maintain respect for the pastoral ministry with which you continue to be associated, even now. You can do this mainly by controlling gossip. The Bible warns against its power to warp behavior of good men (James 3:1–12; Prov. 16:28; 18:8; 26:20). Warn your members against bad-mouthing any Christian church or pastor to anyone, whether believer or nonbeliever.

9. *Trust God and trust the deliberative process.*
   Trust God to make you a better church for the next pastor and the next pastor a better one for you. Trust the process to help you make the transition in a way that rebuilds lost confidence within your church. It takes time, as do all good things.

6

Why Do Forced Exits Happen?

"They happen because preachers keep nailing themselves to crosses of greed and lust," says the media; yet the facts show it's not that simple. What they reveal is rampant infighting and conflict within Protestant congregations today due to contentious groups or individuals. I will substantiate this claim in two ways: first, through the poignant testimony of terminated pastors, whether victims or villains; second, by the evidence of three forced-exit studies spanning a decade.

"If you keep on biting and devouring each other, watch out or you will be destroyed by each other," Paul said in Galatians 5:15. That day has already come for many local churches because the primary reason for church fights is power politics, pure and simple.

Years ago preachers used to get forced out for preaching the gospel. The Lord Jesus was so rejected at Nazareth, his hometown (Luke 4:16–30), and in Jerusalem at the Feast of Tabernacles (John, chapters 7 and 8).

The apostle Paul holds the record for biblical forced exits with four: at Iconium (Acts 14:1–7) he and Barnabas faced a situation sharply divided between those receptive and unreceptive to the gospel, complicated by the skullduggery of a few who sought to abuse them. In Thessalonica (Acts 17:1–10), he and Silas were freed on bond after a mob framed them on charges of treason. In Corinth (Acts 18:1–8), Paul left the synagogue in mid-sermon due to abuse from the listeners and began a house church right next door; and in Jerusalem (where his reputation caught up with him), he was dragged from the temple and beaten severely (Acts 21:27–32). The riot ended only when the "police" arrived.

For Paul and for Jesus, the issue was the message; for many modern-day pastors, the issue is incidental to the power games being played. We asked forcibly terminated pastors to name the reason their lay leaders would give for their exit. The reasons given below fall into ten major categories.

1.	Unfit or stayed too long	28%
2.	Congregational politics or powerful individuals	20%
3.	Divorce/marital difficulties/sexual sin	11%
4.	Doctrinal differences	10%
5.	Finances	8%
6.	Pastoral staff conflict	7%
7.	Incompatibility	6%
8.	Denominational polity/politics	5%
9.	Never learned the reason	4%
10.	Drug or alcohol abuse	1%

NOTE: The next few pages will frequently include the denominational affiliations of forced-out pastors. They are not given to embarrass anyone but to help those denominations accept greater responsibility for this problem. I hope for the reader's understanding, realizing the objectivity of being specific.

Pastor Unfit/Stayed Too Long (28 percent)

We found three types of reasons for pastoral dismissals in this category. Were they justified? You decide, but only after you have read the entire chapter. The first rationale claimed the pastor was either a false teacher or uncalled to ministry. One Foursquare pastor and one Independent Charismatic pastor allegedly fit this description.

The second rationale was unethical conduct. An Assembly of God pastor writes,

> The issue of [my] smoking allowed people (a few) to take a parting shot. The District lined up behind the most vocal people. Their concept was, "Stand with the church, you can always get more preachers." I was not allowed to preach for six months. After one year I am ready to re-enter the market. Again no help from the District.

Third, survey responses demonstrated that pastors are fired for personal reasons—two Lutherans and one Southern Baptist because they weren't friendly enough; an Independent Baptist due to his wife's attitude; a veteran Wesleyan due to the need for a younger man; and a United Methodist pastor for having children and pets in the parsonage. One Presbyterian pastor listed overinvolvement beyond the local church as the cause of his departure. In most of these cases internal political problems in the congregation were accompanying factors.

Are these pastors all unfit, or are some being scape-goated? Seventy-five percent of these "unfit" pastors listed "powerful individuals," "competing power groups in the congregation," "lack of discipline of contentious members" or some other congregational factor as one cause of their forced exit. But which came first: the pastor's alleged incompetence (or excessive tenure), or the in-house politics of the church members?

Warren Wiersbe has written, "I have discovered that lack of respect for spiritual leadership is the main cause for church fights and splits."[1] Could he be right?

Congregational Politics/Powerful Individuals (20 percent)

Verbal responses by pastors fitting into this category exhibited four separate ecclesiastical power games. The most frequently reported subgroup of these political factors is powerful individuals or groups. A Nazarene pastor who has experienced three forced exits says the reason was "political moves by powerful laymen in each case." A Lutheran pastor was shown the door when he opposed a "small group in the church [which] wished to handle a legacy without full approval of the congregation."

The abuse of power by lay leaders appeared most poignantly in three quotations. First, from a United Methodist pastor: "This lady ran the church. For six years I got along with her. Then she said it was time for me to move and I did." Next, a Presbyterian minister: "I went for psychoanalysis to change my personality to become more acceptable to the powerful people in the church. However, because of the stress I could not relax enough." Surely no one could relax while trying to act like a different person. Yet this pastor was willing to try it to please the people on whom he was financially dependent—a tragic situation! An American Baptist pastor wryly observed, "I had one woman who worked against me fourteen years. She was a Bob Jones woman and they are always right."

A second power game had revenge as its motive. A Pentecostal man involved in a co-pastorate said, "The other pastor ran off with the senior deacon's wife and the board 'cleaned house.'"

A third group of responses indicated lingering emotional ties to a previous pastor. A General Baptist minister was forced out due to the fact that "the church had already called back a former pastor because attendance was dropping." A forcibly terminated Presbyterian cleric remarked: "The founding pastor of the church and his family controlled the church."

The fourth group of responses had to do with the failure to maintain clear distinctions between members and nonmembers. An Assembly of God pastor claims that the reason for his forced exit was ". . . lack of numerical growth [yet] there was a failure of the board to cleanse the membership roll. People came to business meetings that never attended while we pastored there." Lay leaders of congregations need to recognize that such blatantly political actions on the part of their brethren are inexcusable and will create further problems.

Divorce/Marital Difficulty/Sexual Sin (11 percent)

We have already noted the case of the Pentecostal co-pastor who was part of the "house cleaning" of the church board when his colleague committed adultery. Other examples came from the Disciples of Christ, Presbyterian, United Methodist, and Christian Reformed denominations.

Doctrine (10 percent)

In two instances charismatic versus noncharismatic rivalries were present. A Presbyterian pastor wrote of his former church, "they would not have allowed me [to come] if they had known my view on tongues." A Disciples of Christ pastor felt used as a scapegoat for his leaders' inability to confront charismatic members who were "wealthy, socially influential, and viewed by lay leaders as unexpendable."

Other cases showed a "denominational/nondenominational" tension, which often amounts to a clash of liberal and conservative theologies. A Lutheran Church Missouri Synod pastor said that his members "[thought I was] trying to make the congregation 'too Lutheran.'" And a pastor who does not identify his former denomination said that a "denominational official told me I used too much Scripture in preaching." In no instance did a pastor report that he was fired for using the Bible too seldom from the pulpit.

Finances (8 percent)

Sixty percent of pastors in this category indicated that internal church problems contributed to the lack of financial support. A terminated Presbyterian pastor puts it succinctly: "We had a lack of funds for an associate pastor after the church had internal problems and loss of members." Another variation on this theme is reflected by the United Methodist associate pastor who reported this: "[The] Pastor/Parish Committee felt [a] need to cut expenses. Their usual procedure was to hire an associate for [only] 2 years so that his salary would not rise above the minimum level."

Pastoral Staff Conflict (7 percent)

Pastors who can't get along with their associates sometimes cloak their ill will in pious or academic rhetoric. Consider this statement from an Independent Church associate pastor: "The senior pastor 'heard from God' that it was time for me to 'be launched into' a more prominent ministerial position [in another church]." A Southern Baptist associate pastor says that he left because his senior pastor "may have been threatened by my education, as he had no seminary background." There's more here than meets the eye.

Incompatibility (6 percent)

There were no comments under this category, evidently because pastors and lay leaders alike felt it was sufficient cause for termination.

Denominational Polity or Politics (5 percent)

These forced exits resulted either from standard procedures requiring resignation or from a form of church governance where a pastor's fate is decided by a superior. One Lutheran cleric stated, "I was an assistant pastor. When my senior pastor resigned, I had to also. This was standard policy in the synod. . . ." An Episcopal rector commented, "[I got] an ultimatum from the bishop for which the lay leadership was never given a reason. . . . To this day, the whole experience is a mystery. No one ever accused me of anything."

The most poignant story of this category came from a young United Methodist pastor whose District Superintendent uprooted him from a thriving parish ministry and thrust him suddenly into a distressed parish whose previous pastor and his paramour (yes, a member) divorced their spouses to marry each other and run away. Though the young pastor did his best to help his new flock recover, their unresolved anger was too great, so he had to leave that new parish as well. Here are two forced exits caused by the poor judgment of one church official. There are advantages to an appointment system; this is one disadvantage.

Never Found Out (4 percent)

One sign of the pastor's extreme vulnerability is the fact that church members as well as denominational officials do not feel obligated to tell him why he has been forced out. Pastors fitting this description came from all kinds of communions, liberal and conservative.

Abuse of Alcohol or Drugs (1 percent)

One pastor indicated that alcohol abuse as well as doubts regarding his call to ministry figured in his forced exit. Given the prevalence of drug abuse in America, other pastors may also struggle with this sin.

Now that you have this evidence in mind, turn your attention to the three major studies that have sought to determine the frequency of various factors causing forced exits. Comparison of them is inexact because the lists of factors vary in size and their definitions occasionally overlap.

In Section D of our questionnaire, we asked the pastor to respond to 24 specific factors involving sin in the congregation or in himself that were causes of his forced exits. These were "Strongly Agree-Agree-Neutral-Disagree-Strongly Disagree" questions with a numerical ranking (5-4-3-2-1, in order). Notice the agreement with the two prior forced-exit studies regarding the top three factors of forced exits:

Table 1
A Comparison of Three Forced-Exit Studies

One can develop a table of "guesstimates" regarding forced exit factors from these three studies by averag-

Respondents:	Pastors		Pastors		Pastors	
Researchers:	Crowell (1990)		Tharp (1984)		Leas (1980)	
	Rank/ Percent		Rank/ Percent		Rank/ Percent	
Powerful minority of members	1	75	1	66		
Conflict of values	2	66	2	26	2	23
Cong. stress or grief	3	61			1	43
Finances	4	31	5	5		
Staff conflicts	4	31	5	5		
Passive leadership	5	26	3	22	3	23
Doctrine	6	25				
Stayed too long/unfit	7	20				
Bossy pastor	8	11	4	12	3	23
Divorce or sex sin	9	10				
No reason given	10	5	5	5		

ing Leas's figures with Tharp's, or Tharp's with Crowell's as the data permits. It looks like this:

Table 2
Estimated Frequencies of Forced-Exit Factors

Category	Percentage
Powerful or warring groups in church	68
Congregational stress	43
Values conflict between members and pastor	27
Poor interpersonal skills or passivity of pastor	24
Authoritarian pastor	17
Pastor stays too long	12
Sexual sin/divorce	11
Doctrine	10
Finances	8
Pastoral staff conflict	7
No reason given	6

The percentages exceed 100 percent obviously, because forced exits in the great majority of cases are due to more than one major factor. Rarely is there only one major cause. The two highest percentages are "powerful or warring groups in the church" and "congregational stress." The third, "poor interpersonal skills or passivity of pastor," could be interpreted to mean that the pastor was fired for his inability to make two groups of bitter rivals coexist peacefully, so that his forced departure was merely a cathartic moment in an ongoing battle.

This, my friend, is the real picture: Not only are too many pastors neck-deep in sin, but we can also say that in many cases their church members are too busy bickering to administer biblical discipline. Fortunately, some denominations are exceptions; but which ones, and why? The next chapter will give you some answers.

7

How Bad Is It?

Which denominations or independent groups have the best track record for preventing forced exits, and why? The questionnaire I mailed to the pastors (see appendix A) provided an opportunity to learn the answer. Its primary goal was to determine whether or not church discipline is a statistically significant factor in reducing the rate of forced pastoral exits.

The results, surprisingly, had nothing to do with liberal or conservative theology. Actual practice seemed more important. Denominations with high percentages of forced-out pastors included both ends of the spectrum: various Churches of God (71 percent), General Baptists (60 percent), various Baptist Bible or Bible Baptist churches (55 percent), American Baptists (40 percent), Disciples of Christ (33 percent), and Independent churches (31 percent). The following chart compares the percentage of survey pastors in each denomination who have served in at least two out of three disciplining churches with the percentage who have experienced forced exits. (A disciplining church is one that emphasizes the fraternal admonition of sinning members in its membership classes, church constitution, and actual practice.) The results from groups with at least five respondents:

Table 3
Discipline and Forced Exits by Denomination

Number Surveyed	Denomination	Discipline Percent	Forced Exits Percent
6	Lutheran, other	66.7	16.7
14	Lutheran Missouri Synod	64.3	15.4
7	Churches of God	42.9	71.4
19	Assembly of God	40.0	26.3
5	Chr. Miss. Alliance	40.0	0.0
11	Indep. Baptists	27.3	27.3
11	Nazarene	27.3	18.2
39	United Methodist	25.0	28.2
24	Presbyterian (PCUSA)	21.7	29.2
11	Episcopal	20.0	18.2
16	Independent	18.8	31.2
30	Ev. Lutheran Ch. America	17.2	23.3
12	Chris. Ch./Chs. of Christ	13.3	0.0
16	American Baptist Con.	12.5	40.0
8	Pentecostal+	12.5	25.0
48	Southern Baptist Con.	10.4	16.7
11	Baptist, other*	10.0	54.5
10	United Ch. of Christ	10.0	25.0
12	Disciples of Christ	0.0	33.3
5	General Baptists	0.0	60.0

#includes these COG's: Anderson, Cleveland, Prophecy, Holiness
+includes Charismatic and Vineyard churches
*includes Bible Baptist, Baptist Bible, and Fundamental Baptist

All pastors were then split into two groups for statistical analysis: those who have served in at least two out of three disciplining churches and those who have not so served. *Pastors in the former group experienced 38 percent fewer forced exits than those in the latter group.* Standard statistical procedures were used to insure that these results were not due to chance.[1] This result shows that church discipline significantly reduces forced pastoral exits, as you can see from Table 4:

Table 4
Forced Exits Relative to Disciplining Churches

Number of Forced Exits	Pastors serving in fewer than 2 out of 3 disciplining chs.		Pastors serving in at least 2 out of 3 disciplining chs.	
	Number/Percent		Number/Percent	
0	218	72	65	83
1	62	21	10	13
2 or more	21	7	3	4
Totals	301	100	78	100

One out of every four pastors had experienced at least one forced exit. Of the pastors who had, 75 percent had endured only one. That's the silver lining in this cloud.

Why the great difference among denominations? National staff members of ten denominations offered their ideas.[2] They blamed the high expectations congregations have for pastors or the pastors' hesitancy to discuss the problem. One said a lack of hierarchical authority allows churches too much liberty in firing pastors. A Lutheran leader speculated that their high doctrine of pastoral "call" helped reduce forced exits. A leader in the General Association of General Baptists wrote, "We do not have this kind of information available [on forced exits in the denomination]. However, I suspect our churches would fall into the category of 'average.'"[3] (Table 3 shows that 60 percent of their respondents were forced out. That's far above average, but is it typical? Until they do their own study, they'll never know.)

A United Methodist national staff member wrote this: "I do not doubt that local church discipline, warring groups and contentious members may be contributing factors to a decision about exiting, and the influence of such factors should not be underestimated."[4] Here is one leader willing to learn from the facts. Are there others?

Could the present oversupply of clergy be a major factor in forced pastoral exits? Brooks Faulkner suggests that a 1980 study indicates a "buyer's market" for churches with a corresponding "pick of the litter" mentality regarding the procurement of new pastors.[5] However, a closer inspection of Faulkner's source shows the authors suggesting the opposite: clergy oversupply creates limitations on mobility, actually reducing a pastor's desire to move by increasing his competition.[6] Which interpretation is true?

To answer this question, I used data from fifteen denominations in my survey. Taking the percentage of forced-out pastors in each communion, I obtained an ordained-clergy-to-church ratio from the *1990 Yearbook of American and Canadian Churches* by simple division, then graphed the effect of the clergy-church ratio on the rate of forced exits. The results indicate that as the number of ordained clergy per church increases, the percentage of force-outs decreases very slightly. The data, however, are widely scattered, as Table 5 shows:

Table 5
Clergy/Church Ratios and Forced Exits

Denomination	C/C Ratio	Forced Exits Percent
United Methodist Church	.98	28.2
American Baptist	1.26	40.0
Christian Missionary All.	1.31	0.0
Baptist, other (average)	1.32	54.5
Churches of God	1.34	71.4
Lutheran Missouri Synod	1.34	15.4
Evang. Luth. Ch. America	1.45	23.3
United Church of Christ	1.58	25.0
Disciples of Christ	1.59	33.3
Presbyterian Church (PCUSA)	1.65	29.2
General Baptist	1.70	60.0
Nazarene	1.70	18.2
Southern Baptist Convention	1.70	16.6
Episcopal	1.84	18.2
Assembly of God	2.46	26.3

Granted we're looking at only one factor here so our conclusions must be tentative. Yet at first glance it does appear that clergy oversupply does not increase forced exits. Rather, clergy oversupply seems to diminish the pastor's hankering to move far more than it serves to increase the congregation's desire to fire him so they may pick from a new "crop" of contenders.

Some, like good capitalists, would attribute forced pastoral exits to laws of supply and demand. If only the problem were that simple! Then we could discourage enough prospective seminarians to increase the demand for pastors. Then churches would hire them more carefully, keep them longer, and probably pay them higher salaries.

Yet all the statistical and verbal data gathered so far point clearly in a spiritual direction. They tell us collectively that it's time for the church to get its house in order. Pastors who behave disgracefully should not be free merely to pack their bags and move on to a new, unsuspecting church to repeat their sins. Similarly contentious and dictatorial church members should not be allowed to chew up and spit out one pastor after another, while their fellow members sit back in frustrated, silent acquiescence.

For many Protestant fellowships, forced exits *are* a problem. How have the churches handled them? How should they?

8

The Trouble with Conflict Management

This chapter will summarize the major insights of conflict theory and then indicate some ways in which its social scientific assumptions clash with biblical principles that should preeminently govern Christian behavior.

Concerted efforts of psychologists and sociologists in this field *have* borne some good fruit. They have shown us that conflict is of several different kinds, has predictable stages of intensity, and requires certain skills to resolve.

Conflict begins when an action by one party is perceived to be threatening to another party who then mounts a protective reaction.[1] This inaugurates a "conflict cycle," which may lead progressivly to resentment, confusion of motives, and confrontation unless preventative action is taken.[2]

Whether individuals, groups, or nations are involved, conflicts fall into one of six categories:

1. Real (A genuine problem correctly perceived)
2. Contingent (Solution exists but is unperceived)
3. Displaced (Conflict over the wrong issue)
4. Misattributed (Conflict between wrong parties)
5. Latent (Hidden or repressed conflict)
6. False (Having no basis, like prejudice)[3]

The Tools of Conflict Management

Certain skills, it is claimed, are necessary to make conflict constructive rather than destructive. Deutsch lists four: *creative thinking; cooperative problem solving; benevolent misperception which minimizes differences without trivializing them;* and *cooperative commitment.*[4] The conflict manager must use his skills to generate valid and useful information about the core issues, to allow free and informed choice regarding the possibility of collaboration or compromise for each issue, and to motivate personal commitment to any agreements that may be reached by the involved parties.[5]

Numerous congregations have been helped by these insights as skilled, trained practitioners applied them to polarized situations. I do not wish to minimize the value of this in the least. All the same, isn't it strange that nearly twenty years and many books after the cry for "better conflict management" was sounded throughout Protestantism, the problem of forced pastoral exits has persisted—and even increased?[6]

What is wrong? Why haven't these valuable insights into conflict management made the impact on churches that they ought by all rights to have made?

The answer is twofold. First, the attempt to use techniques developed in the "value-free" world of social science aided the spread of an overly tolerant attitude toward sin in Protestant churches. Second, this attempt to implement conflict management techniques ignored the truth obvious to every seasoned parent that negotiation is impossible without discipline or the threat of it.

Life Has Rules Too

To illustrate, consider the situation of a family with an "incorrigibly" rebellious child used to getting his own way. His parents will be able to negotiate with him only after his rebellion is punished. Furthermore, the child will have to signify by his acceptance of punishment that he is willing to negotiate. Then potential for progress may appear. Why? Rules of negotiation depend on rules of behavior *per se.* The conflict manager who fails to recognize this truth will find that even the negotiation process may be used as a tool by a rebellious individual within any group, especially the church. To prevent such a misfortune, other foundational rules must already be in effect governing group behavior. Just as a drowning man cannot suddenly begin learning to swim, so a rebellious man cannot suddenly begin to learn cooperation in a conflict. It is naive to think otherwise.

A Theory Without Standards

Now we turn to the prior claim that the "value-free" ethos of conflict management theory has aided the spreading tolerance of sin in Protestant churches. While many other factors are also involved, such as secularism and family decline, the failure of conflict management to proscribe certain behaviors renders it less effective in reducing conflict within the local church.

Two theoretical tendencies in conflict management theory arising from its academic origins are relativism and humanism. Within industry or government these tendencies would not create so much role confusion, but within the church they only aid the tactics of divisive and contentious individuals.

For example, what happens when seated around the bargaining table are several different styles of conflict management—let's say, one person willing to compromise within limits; two wanting peace at any price; one seeking victory at any cost; and one hoping to make collaborators of everyone? Who rules? At this vital point, the value-free nature of the discipline abandons us to our own devices. Nor does it offer any guidance as to when compromise in negotiation would entail compromise with sin. Conflict management has little to say about how the content of issues should affect the mediation approach to take.

The relativism inherent in conflict management is revealed in its assumption that no one group has more authority or truth than another in the conflict. G. Douglass Lewis quotes the Lord's command to love our enemies and adds, "[T]o love another is to affirm the right and necessity of that person . . . to have a unique perspective. . . . God's love is all-inclusive."[7]

True enough; but having a right to my opinion doesn't *make* my opinion right. As a Christian my right to hold a different opinion ends where God has spoken in the Bible. Yet conflict management authors give the clear impression that to avoid the cardinal sin of prejudice, every opinion must in principle be considered equally valid. This neither prevents conflict nor shortens board meetings.

The humanistic orientation of conflict management theory appears in its absence of any God-centered analysis of the roots of conflict. Its experts tell us that "stress," or "change," or "man's purposive nature" are the causes. They warn us that conflict is not necessarily sinful, yet fail to say that it often is. Speaking half the truth is sometimes as bad as speaking none. Again, you will seldom find in conflict theory a word about conscience, conviction, or confession of sin. To encourage such would be to "impose" one's values on another. Ultimately, however, no conflict is ever ended without such an imposition. Someone must win, if only the conflict manager himself who seeks to have just as much influence as any other party to the discussion. No one's position is "value free"; the only question is "Whose values shall we accept?"

The result of this incipient relativism and humanism is that no norms have been established to govern the interaction of conflict management with spiritual authority in the local congregation. The experts have failed to see that rules of negotiation depend on rules of proper behavior, which in turn depend on commonly held beliefs.

This omission is serious, not incidental. It minimizes the fickleness of the human heart which makes so many compromises uneasy, unstable, and temporary. It ignores the call to search our own hearts for unrealistic expectations and instead encourages them to be disguised as "needs." It ignores the biblical mandate for church members to submit to those in authority over them, substituting for obedience an indefinite, open-ended process, subject to manipulation by anyone in the congregation who bellows loudly enough. A corrupt heart will corrupt any process of negotiation unless there is firm, loving, and consistent enforcement of behavioral boundaries.

No wonder so many churches are frustrated! Everyone's seeking to grab the rudder and steer. It can't go on much longer. The answer is *discipline.*

9

Toughlove Applied to Churches and Pastors

Whether they like it or not churches must discipline to survive. This chapter offers practical help for those new to the concept. But first—another story.

Fifteen years ago family counselors Phyllis and David York had a problem: They seemed to be able to help other people's kids but had trouble with their own. Reasoning, negotiation, compromise, and placating behavior didn't work. With accession to each demand, their teenage daughters demanded more.

Then Phyllis and David began to get tough. They set rules and punished disobedience, using penalties like forbidding use of the family car, limiting phone calls, and refusing to intervene when their daughters had run-ins with authorities. They made an agreement with their neighbors: If the York children defied curfew, a sign would be posted on the door of their home saying, "You are not welcome here. Go to the neighbors' until your return can be negotiated." The Yorks promised to reciprocate if their neighbors had to do the same with their kids. Then something strange happened: The kids began to shape up—all of them. So the Yorks began training other parents to do likewise in a program they called "Toughlove." It now has over 150 branches nationwide.

What helped save the York family was merely the application of old-fashioned discipline—whether they realized it or not. Curiously it is highly unpopular to advocate that churches ought to practice discipline as well. Mention the word and you are immediately relegated to the lunatic fringe of Christianity.

Yet churches *are* families. They have composite personalities constituted by the personalities of their members. Like a family they need to nurture their members, loving them enough to tell them when their behavior is inappropriate and doing something about it.

Why are we so hesitant to discipline in the church? Many of us don't know how to do it; some have been victimized by its abuses. Most of us, I suspect, fear that disciplined people will either leave the church or retaliate in vengeance. My prayer is that when you finish this final chapter, none of these reasons will deter you.

A Study in Contrasts

What does a nondisciplining church have to gain by implementing biblical discipline of sinning members or pastors? Let's use some actual cases to illustrate the difference. Although these cases were carefully selected to emphasize the difference that discipline makes, the statistical data from the survey tends to support the generalizations that will be drawn from these instances. We start with two cases from nondisciplining churches:

Case One: The Panhandling Preacher

George was a personable young pastor and an excellent preacher. His new congregation felt fortunate that he accepted the job. What they didn't know was that George had been well schooled in panhandling. The senior pastor of George's previous church owed that congregation thirty-five thousand dollars from loans to make payments on real-estate property that he couldn't sell. George must have learned something from him, for on arriving in his new church, George asked repeatedly for loans and cash advances above his salary and was able to obtain ten thousand dollars over and above his earnings in his first year at the 130-member congregation.

George also told his new flock that he was having difficulty selling his old residence. One member donated money from his part-time retirement job to help him make the payments. Then it was learned that George also owed $8,300 on a $15,000 private loan he obtained from a retiree in his former church. Because he said he was filing for bankruptcy, George asked his new church to co-sign a note for the amount or else the retiree might become an unsecured creditor.

When two leaders in his new church learned of his cajoling for money, they confronted him, and he became very angry. The rest of the church leaders sat back passively, confused about their role and hesitant to get involved. The confronting members left the church and the church board considered the problem solved.

But there was one problem: The church treasurer had written George some checks for salary advances without the knowledge of the trustees. In fact the trustees were never fully aware of the total amount of money George had received from all sources, including the denomination! When the congregation's president and vice-president learned of these improprieties, they refused to attend the annual congregational meeting. A year later George resigned, yet the church has taken no action either to tighten financial procedures within the congregation or to examine pastoral candidates more thoroughly.

Case Two: Senior Pastor Piranha

Sam came to his new church with a "gentleman's agreement" that within six months the senior pastor would retire and elevate Sam to be his successor. That agreement changed when the senior pastor noticed that the members preferred Sam's preaching to his own. Feeling threatened he began to spread lies about Sam which, when they were discovered, caused the senior pastor to burst into tears at a board meeting over lack of support from his lay leaders. The board didn't press the issue. Later the senior pastor suspended Sam for three days on a false charge, covering it up by telling the church that Sam had asked for three days off to do "sightseeing." By that time Sam and his wife were ready to move. They were told soon after that there were enough votes in the church to oust the senior pastor and vote him in, but Sam refused that maneuver. Senior Pastor Piranha is still at that church and has forced out another associate under much the same circumstances.

Why do nondisciplining churches seem unable to deal with their problems? They lack the skill, knowledge, desire, procedure, or authority to do so. In some cases the goal is not the resolution of conflict but the avoidance of responsibility. Thus every church leader who is not immediately involved in the conflict runs for cover. The little fish swim to safety while the piranha dominate.

How Disciplining Churches Function

Although a "disciplining" church is not a "trouble-free" church, it is able to contain the damage which con-

tentious members or leaders may often cause. Once
again, let's look at two cases.

Case One: A Unified Church Board

An Assembly of God pastor from the Midwest wrote:

> I have, in the past 14 months, dealt with an individual in
> my church that precipitated the departure of 4–5 fami-
> lies. All of these were close friends of the individual
> that had to be dealt with. However, I was supported by
> strong leadership in the church and we did not com-
> promise or bow to the "desire to control" the church by
> these people. They tried very hard to destroy the church
> and its ministry in our community. However, we stood
> firm and continued with the vision of the church. We
> did not try to retaliate or engage in debate with these
> people. It has been hard, but God has helped us through
> and brought healing to our church.

Naturally one cannot capture all the nuances of
church infighting in one summary paragraph. Perhaps
the pastor is leaving out some uncomplimentary details
concerning his own position. But if we assume that the
church board was justified in standing with him against
his critics—and the statistical data tends to be in favor of
that assumption—then another disruptive battle was
averted due to unanimity among the spiritual leadership of the congregation.

Case Two: Wanting Blood, Not Repentance

Bob is an energetic pastor whose zeal came across as
insensitivity to 33 of his 325 fellow members who
approached 2 church board members with their griev-
ances. The board members relayed the dissatisfaction
to Pastor Bob. (In line with Matthew 18:15, the dissi-
dents should have gone to him themselves.) Pastor Bob,
after devoting two weeks to self-examination and prayer,

issued a statement to the congregation confessing his sin, asking time for his own personal growth and healing in the church, and thanking everyone for their willingness to speak the truth in love to him.

But they didn't live happily ever after, for the disgruntled members wouldn't settle for repentance. They wanted Bob to get out. Five months later the malcontents drafted a letter to the church board calling for a vote of confidence. What follows is a portion of the board's carefully worded reply:

> The board holds all of you in high regard. We confess we have been displeased with some of the actions that we have seen and some of the things that we have heard, but that has not caused us to think of you as less than God thinks of you. We confess we have come close to becoming your accusers. God has worked in us to not become judgmental toward you. Though at times that wasn't easy, we have attempted to allow God to have His way in us.
>
> With these things in mind, we have talked about the call for a vote of confidence in relation to [Bob] as pastor. . . . This board has decided that this course of action would produce an environment for further confusion and make the way for greater division within the congregation. . . . We also do not see hard evidence of improper conduct or wrongdoing to warrant such a vote. . . . The personal traits of Pastor [Bob] have been described to him in the areas where correction is needed. . . . He has responded in a proper manner and that is sufficient.

When the board refused to bend, thirty members left the church and went as a group to a neighboring church whose pastor permitted them to remain a power group in exile. From their new base of operation, the dissident members remained a fellowship to themselves, identifying and influencing vulnerable families back in their former congregation. Their continued politicking finally led Pastor Bob to resign a year later. Had Bob and his fellow leaders received help from the neighboring church, the discipline would have worked. Instead this case changed from a success story to a failure (during the process of writing this book) due to the opportunism of one fellow pastor.

Decisive action by disciplining churches resolves problems and helps to prevent their recurrence if leaders receive the necessary moral support. Faced with legitimate authority, contentious members or pastors come to recognize that their disruptive tactics won't work, unless they can find a church where "anything goes." If they are able to do so, discipline will often fail. If not, "An ounce of prevention is worth a pound of cure."

Prerequisites for Discipline

Biblical church discipline has six prerequisites which we will examine in order:

1. The right church
2. The right authority
3. The right cause
4. The right leaders
5. The right method
6. The right spirit

The Right Church

You can't establish discipline in a church filled with "Sunday-morning Christians." There must be high personal commitment to Jesus Christ as the Lord of each individual's life. Jesus said, "My sheep listen to my voice; I know them, and they follow me" (John 10:27). While an unbeliever can play the "church game" for a time, he cannot live peacefully and intelligently within a truly spiritual fellowship. First Corinthians 2:14a says: "The man without the Spirit does not accept the things that come from the Spirit of God, for they are foolishness to him." Such pretenders create strife within the church simply because they seek their own will, not God's. Jude 19 says, "These are the men who divide you, who follow mere natural instincts and do not have the Spirit."

The Right Authority

"My church board gave me a hard time until I told them I'd invoke the Book of Discipline on them. Then they backed off." So spoke a Methodist pastor to me several years ago, thinking he had won a great victory by "pulling rank" on his members. He seemed unaware that he had only encouraged them to turn the tables on him at the next opportunity! Irrespective of the organizational justification for constitutions, committees, and church courts, it is imperative that discipline find its supreme authority in the Bible, the Word of God, applied to a sinning believer's life by those who know him best—fellow members who have supported and loved him and his family, thus earning the right to confront him in Christ's name.

The Right Cause

Which sins will you discipline? *All* of them? It's impossible! True, it's impossible to discipline every sin but it should also be unnecessary, for Christians can confess most sins directly to God. Only when they are overtaken in a sin—caught in its grip—or when they are unaware of their sin should discipline be necessary. Yet which sins merit it? Adultery? Child abuse? Drunkenness? Lying? Cheating? Swearing? Overeating? Shoplifting? Where is the line to be drawn?

Roman Catholic theology distinguishes between degrees of sins in its penitential system. Some evangel-

ical Protestant churches have a shorter "catalog of sins."
Typically failure to contribute to the church, divorce,
and adultery are disciplined consistently while all other
sins go ignored. How can discipline be consistent?

J. Carl Laney suggests guidelines by which church
leaders can exercise discipline without excessive accu-
sation of fellow members or inconsistency:

> The sins which necessitate church discipline can be
> divided into four major categories: *Violations of Chris-
> tian love, unity, law and truth.* Violations of *love* would
> include private offenses against a brother or sister (cf.
> Matt. 5:23–24). Violations of Christian *unity* would be
> divisive actions which destroy the peace of the church
> (Rom. 16:17; Titus 3:10). Violations of Christian *law* or
> morality would involve the breaking of such ethical
> codes and guidelines as are set forth in the Old and New
> Testaments. . . . Violations of Christian *truth* would
> involve the rejection of essential doctrines of the faith—
> heresy (1 Tim. 6:3–5; Titus 3:9–10; 2 John 7–11).[1]

Why should Christians watch each other's behavior?
Colossians 1:28 yields the answer: "We proclaim him,
admonishing and teaching everyone with all wisdom,
so that we may present everyone perfect in Christ." The
price for spiritual maturity is discipline. Where self-
discipline is lacking, the body of Christ must intervene
to protect the sinner from himself so that he will not
suffer the Lord's chastening or dishonor his Savior.

To summarize, the right cause for church discipline is
the advancement of Christian maturity by correcting the
sin which threatens the integrity of a local fellowship
of Christian believers. One cannot avoid our Lord's command to discipline with the excuse, "I love rather than
judge" because indifference is not love. Similarly one
cannot plead false modesty: "I too am a sinner, and who
am I to say who has sinned?" because as John Howard

Yoder points out, the duty to forgive does not depend on one's own sinlessness.[2] Jesus says explicitly (Matt. 6:12–15) that those who are forgiven *must* also forgive.

The Right Leaders

Without exception, the New Testament qualifications for local church leadership have to do with character, not business expertise or political influence. In a word leaders must be *godly*. This is essential if they are to make decisions according to the Bible rather than "how we do it" at XYZ Corporation.

The appointment of elders is more a spiritual than a political process. In Acts 14:23 we are told that Paul and Barnabas ["appointed" elders; the Greek word *cheirotoneo* used there means careful selection, not ordination by laying on of hands or voting. The New Testament shows that a man is appointed to elder after demonstration of his desire to serve (1 Tim. 3:1), his qualifications (vv. 1–7; Titus 1:5–9) and after passing examination (1 Tim. 3:10; 5:22–25).

The two lists of character qualifications given in the Scriptures show a remarkable similarity:

1 Timothy 3:	Titus 1:
Above reproach	Blameless
Husband of one wife	Husband of one wife
Temperate	Obedient, believing children
Self-controlled	Not overbearing
Respectable	Not quick-tempered
Hospitable	Not given to much wine
Able to teach	Not violent
Not given to much wine	No dishonest gain
Not violent but gentle	Hospitable
Not quarrelsome	Lover of good
Not a lover of money	Self-controlled

Manage his own family well	Upright, holy, and disciplined
Have obedient children	Holding firmly to Bible teaching
Not a recent convert	
Good reputation among the nonChristians	

Why such stringent qualifications? First, leaders should function as a team, so they must be temperate and not quarrelsome. Second, they have the serious responsibility to decide what sins require discipline and to begin the process of individual reproof when necessary; thus they must be able to teach the Scriptures and have no unrepented or uncorrected sin in their lives. Third, since the congregation is expected to submit to them, leaders' worthy examples must be reflected in the emotional and spiritual health of their families. Fourth, since contentious members in the church will attempt to manipulate them and lead them into compromise, leaders must be able to hold fast to scriptural teaching. Fifth, since they must be rightly motivated for discipline, having only the desire to see a fellow Christian grow, leaders must be free from love of money, and lovers of all that is good. Once you understand what leaders must do, the necessary qualifications seem quite logical.

Tolerance of leaders who have abandoned these qualifications by falling into sin will create a growing tolerance of sin in the church, as John MacArthur observes:

> Where did we get the idea that a year's leave of absence can restore integrity to someone who has squandered his reputation and destroyed people's trust? Certainly not from the Bible. Trust forfeited is not so easily regained. . . . What about forgiveness? Shouldn't we be eager to restore our fallen brethren? To fellowship, yes; but not to leadership. It is not an act of love to return a

disqualified man to public ministry. It is an act of disobedience.

By all means we should be forgiving. But we cannot
erase the consequences of sin. I am not advocating that
we "shoot our own wounded." I'm simply saying that
we shouldn't rush them back to the front lines. . . . Doing
so is unbiblical and lowers the standard God has set.[3]

This is very strong medicine. But in a church so sick
with sin that society mocks its leaders, we must acknowl-
edge the need for immediate, drastic treatment.

While many churches consider these demands impossible for laypersons, they expect any pastoral candidate
to exhibit many of these godly qualities! Alexander
Strauch sets the challenge plainly before the church
today:

> *Spiritual laziness is a major reason why most churches
> will never establish a biblical eldership.* Men are more
> than willing to let someone else fulfill their spiritual
> responsibilities. . . . Many people say, "You can't expect
> men to raise their families, work all day, and provide
> leadership for the local church." But that is simply not
> true. . . . I've seen people build and remodel houses in
> their spare time.[4]

How do we train godly men? One pastor has a church
of young believers who have never chosen a leadership
board. The men are meeting weekly for Bible study and
discipleship, which includes one-to-one accountability
for one's complete life in thought, word, and action.
That's a good start which will lead to the selection of
leaders. The next ingredient for church discipline is a
key one.

The Right Method

If your brother sins against you, go and show him his fault, just between the two of you. If he listens to you, you have won your brother over. But if he will not listen, take one or two others along, so that "every matter may be established by the testimony of two or three witnesses." If he refuses to listen to them, tell it to the church; and if he refuses to listen even to the church, treat him as you would a pagan or a tax collector (Matt. 18:15–17).

The method of discipline prescribed by the Lord Jesus Christ, the risen head of the church, has four successive stages, each one building on the other and offering to the Christian caught in sin the option of repentance, restoration, and renewed integrity. Much helpful instruction is packed into these three verses. Our careful attention will be richly rewarded as we examine these stages of church discipline.

> Stage One: Private conversation
> Stage Two: A conference with witnesses
> Stage Three: Tell it to the church
> Stage Four: Redemptive excommunication

Stage One: Private Conversation

"*If* your brother sins against you . . ." the Lord says. One reason for private conversation is that you may find that you didn't know all the facts and that your brother did not sin against you. That provides you with the opportunity to repent of any false charges or unworthy thoughts you may have held. No matter who has sinned, it's better to find out in private than in a committee meeting. Such action demonstrates respect for another's privacy and integrity.

The clear expectation is that we are to go directly to the one who may have sinned—not to any third party to gossip or enlist supporters for our cause, for that diminishes the possibility of reconciliation.

The goal of the private meeting is also stated by the Lord Jesus. He desires us, when all is said and done, to have "won your brother over"; not to our side, but to the Lord's side again; not to a more congenial point of view, but to a life of Christian fellowship and service. Nothing less has an intention of redemptive love.

This private meeting is not to be misconstrued as mildly therapeutic and innocuous conversation. In it the sin must be revealed. The word for *show* in *show him his fault* is *elenchō,* which means "expose to the light." Paul did this with Peter when he tiptoed on the border of heresy (Gal. 2:11). Did Peter hold this against Paul for the rest of his life? Hardly; for in 2 Peter 3:15 he calls Paul "our dear brother." He accepted and profited from the discipline of a fellow apostle. How much more should we accept a word of correction from a fellow believer!

Only if there is no repentance whatsoever on the brother's part can the next step be taken. It is:

Stage Two: A Conference with Witnesses

In requiring "two or three witnesses," the Lord is doing far more than adapting an Old Testament law for use in the New Testament church. True, Deuteronomy 19:15 enshrined this rule as protection against perjury toward an innocent man. Yet there's more to be done.

In the first place, someone must make certain that the fraternal discipline is being conducted with the right spirit (see next section). Is the confronter attempting to force a confession or to threaten and cajole the accused brother? Or is the accused brother's hostility and unre-

pentant attitude preventing any progress? Only independent witnesses can answer those important questions accurately.

Second, if an accused brother needs to confess his
sin, yet is unwilling to recognize it, more pressure needs
to be applied. He needs to see that his sin indirectly
affects all Christians everywhere. The witnesses chosen
from his own church fellowship testify to the fact that "a
little yeast works through the whole batch of dough" (1
Cor. 5:6), and that the church needs to be purified from
corrupting and distorting influences. So often today sin
is justified with the idea that there is a magic sphere of
privacy protecting part of our lives and that what we
do in it is our own business. The Bible tells us something different: "You are not your own; you were bought
at a price. . . . honor God" (1 Cor. 6:19–20a).

Stage Three: Tell It to the Church

If the sinning Christian remains unrepentant in front
of two or three witnesses, the Lord commands us to "tell
it to the church." His words must be understood very
precisely because some congregations have suffered
defamation of character suits by their own members
in attempting to carry out this directive, as discussed
earlier.

First, what should be told to the church? Some pastors argue that at this stage only the sin (not the person's name) should be mentioned. While confidentiality
is admirable, at this stage the person's name must be
mentioned if the congregation is to be mobilized in calling that person to repentance. I consider this the only
justifiable purpose of informing the church. It is simply
inconceivable that the Lord would require a bare for-
mality just to "post notice" before excommunication. If
anything the person's name should be mentioned but

the nature of the sin omitted. Lawyers Lynn Buzzard and Thomas Brandon, Jr., suggest this announcement:

> It has come to the attention of the board that a member of our church must be dealt with by church discipline. The church board has carefully and thoroughly investigated the facts and has confirmed that discipline is necessary. . . . The Board [has] appealed to the one who has sinned. All attempts have so far been rejected. Scripture now instructs us to inform the church so that the united prayer and obedience of the members to the scriptural steps of discipline may be used of God to bring this person to repentance and to a life of victory over sin. Before naming this person we are asking each member to set aside a time of personal self-examination. . . . We are doing this so that Satan will be given no opportunity to bring confusion or division in this matter and that God may be free, because of our obedience, to accomplish his purposes in the life of the one who has sinned.[5]

Church leaders and pastors who practice biblical discipline know well that sinning Christians frequently resign from membership or leave the fellowship before this stage. Certainly they have that privilege, although their intentions in doing so are often questionable. How then should the church respond?

At first only the local congregation should be informed of the member's resignation. Some churches become vulnerable to lawsuits when in correspondence to neighboring churches they publicize a member's sin—even if their intent is to invite cooperation in biblical discipline! It is better, if necessary, to notify the sinner's new "church of refuge" in this way:

> Dear Pastor: This is to inform you that (name) has resigned and left our fellowship as one consequence of

disciplinary proceedings against [him]. We cannot recommend [him] to you as a member[s] in good standing
and urge you to counsel [him] in such a way as to lead
[him] to repentance and renewed fellowship with Jesus
Christ. (Signed)

However, don't be prepared to give up too easily. If
rebellious or unrepentant members stop attending but
have not yet joined another church, they remain under
your care until they covenant with another congregation. This fact should be emphasized vigorously with
new members so they know just how seriously your
church takes membership.

Stage Four: Redemptive Excommunication

"Redemptive Excommunication" is Marlin Jeschke's
apt term for Jesus' command to treat the unrepentant
sinner "as you would a pagan or a tax collector." Jeschke
describes this act of excommunication as "the form
under which the church continues to extend the gospel
to the impenitent."[6]

Until the very moment of excommunication, the person under discipline should have opportunity to receive
communion. Jesus did not exclude Judas from the Last
Supper, although he knew what was in his mind;
instead, he offered him a piece of bread as a last gesture
of grace (John 13:26). Verse 27 plainly shows that Judas
did not take it intending to change his ways.

However, once excommunication takes place, the
church must act with extreme circumspection toward
the person under discipline lest common casualness
conceal the sin that has harmed fellowship in Christ.
Avoidance of the person must take place to a sufficient
degree that the silent call for repentance is felt. The bal-
ance is struck in 2 Thessalonians 3:14–15, where social-

izing is restricted, yet some verbal communication is permitted to maintain a word of warning about sin.

I agree with Jeschke that excommunication does not force a husband to avoid his wife, or vice versa; for Scripture plainly teaches in 1 Corinthians 7:10–17 that a believing spouse can have a redemptive influence on his or her mate. However let us not delude ourselves into thinking that either member of a married couple can long avoid having to confess his or her sin; what affects us in the spiritual realm touches every aspect of our lives, including the most intimate and domestic ones.

Research indicates that less than half of all discipline cases end in restoration. Hence this last prerequisite may be the most crucial one.

The Right Spirit

The key verse here is Galatians 6:1: "Brothers, if someone is caught in a sin, you who are spiritual should restore him gently." The word for "gently" is a form of the same word the Lord Jesus used for "meek" in Matthew 5:5. We must go to the sinner with a humble spirit.

Such a meek spirit is admirably demonstrated by Paul, who advised the Corinth church not to "rub in" the punishment of discipline for sin given to an errant brother:

> The punishment inflicted on him by the majority is sufficient for him. Now instead, you ought to forgive and comfort him, so that he will not be overwhelmed by excessive sorrow. I urge you, therefore, to reaffirm your love for him (2 Cor. 2:6–8).

It is the church's attitude of love for the sinner that conveys the message that its discipline and its living of the gospel belong naturally together. The same love that calls the lost sinner to new life in Christ refuses to abandon him when he lapses back into sin.

The Discipline of Leaders

Ministers are not immune to sinful rebellion against their Lord. Nor is Scripture ignorant of this possibility. Therefore, we conclude with a look at the disciplinary process for sinning Christian leaders (lay or ordained), and with some suggestions for how to begin implementing biblical discipline in your church if you have not already practiced it.

The process of discipline for a sinning leader closely parallels that for a regular member of the fellowship. A private meeting takes place, and in case there are questions regarding the commission of the alleged sin, two or three witnesses are required (1 Tim. 5:19–20). The leader is treated somewhat more harshly in that his or her sin is told publicly to the congregation in the context of a public rebuke from the other church leaders (v. 20). This is expressly to maintain a sense of reverence for God's holiness and sin's great price.

With regard to the restoration of a sinning leader to fellowship, all are agreed: "Yes!" But there is disagreement regarding the possibility of restoration to leadership. Some highly respected Bible teachers of national repute (John MacArthur, Jack Wyrtzen[7]) say that fallen leaders cannot be so restored; others (J. Carl Laney[8]) leave the possibility open. This is a decision each church must make. It cannot be made with the lighthearted tolerance of sin found in previous decades. The church's shame is too great for that now.

If restoration to leadership is allowed, it would seem wise to give sufficient time for the former minister to demonstrate a life which truly honors God. This would typically require several years. As lesser and humbler opportunities to serve are willingly accepted and fulfilled, restoration continues.

Is the Church Ready for It?

Geddes MacGregor wrote, "The relaxation of discipline has often more absurd results than ever attended its excesses." There are some encouraging signs (and some warning signs) that churches in America are waking up to the need for biblical discipline. One encouraging sign—the Evangelical Lutheran Church in America has adopted guidelines for disciplining pastors. Grounds for disciplinary action include substance abuse, sexual abuse, and misuse of church funds. ELCA general counsel David Hardy says that without such guidelines, "we are going to be abdicating to the civil courts what constitutes proper conduct of pastors."

On the other hand, one warning sign comes from the Roman Catholic Church where many Catholics no longer go to confession. Bishops say the reason for this twenty-five-year trend of decline is "a less pervasive sense of sin." Laity claim they obtain "reconciliation by other means."

Clearly, sin has crept into the Christian camp to such a degree that sporadic "crackdowns" on backslidden members or pastors alone will fail to do the job. An ongoing, consistent, scriptural method of discipline must be in place at all times, administered by godly leaders, to restrain Christians from dishonoring the Lord and to restore them gently if they fall. This process must apply equally to leaders and members and must be conducted in an impartial yet redemptive manner. All this must happen without overloading an already weary church bureaucracy with its overworked executives or straining already tight budgets.

What could be more obvious? Discipline the Bible way: at the local church level, with godly leaders, with gentleness, and with the authority of Scripture as our guide.

But are local congregations ready to handle this responsibility? In the survey one out of every four pastors said they neither follow Christ's rule of discipline nor make themselves accountable to fellow Christians. That is not a reassuring sign.

On the other hand it appears that pastors aren't getting much support in discipline from their lay leaders either. Gordon Schroeder's survey of 130 theologically conservative pastors revealed that most of them felt their congregations were doing either "fair" (39 percent) or "poor" (18 percent) when it comes to church discipline. Only 31 percent of them rated their churches "good" and 12 percent "excellent."[9]

Schroeder's survey also shows that church discipline definitely is not carried out to an extreme: Of the approximately 26,000 people involved in the congregations of the surveyed pastors, only 70 had been removed from membership for disciplinary reasons.[10] That's certainly not excessive by any standard.

Are local churches ready to accept discipline? Not yet. Many more pastors and lay leaders must see the need, read the Word, and respond in obedience to Jesus Christ. We need a far greater love for God and a far greater revulsion to sin than we now have. Most of all we need a gentle spirit in dealing with the sinner rather than our modern, jaded tolerance or shallow, hypocritical moralism.

How can we ever begin to require more of our members without causing utter rebellion and controversy? Good question. Decades of backsliding aren't easily or quickly corrected. Try these suggestions from Marlin Jeschke for a quick start in the right direction:

1. Begin with a study of what it means to be a follower of Jesus Christ.
2. Establish meaningful membership in your congregation and denomination.
3. Inaugurate a congregational policy for discipline with clear rules.
4. Take the next need for discipline that arises and tackle it with love.[11]

Let's expand the first three points beginning with the need to study. A godly wife and mother in our church was explaining to a young woman the connection between faith and obedience using the Lord's words in John 15:14, "'You are my friends if you do what I command.'" The young woman answered, "Yes, but didn't he mean, To keep the Ten Commandments'?" She didn't realize that those who follow Jesus Christ must seek to live by every word that comes from him.

Fortunately there are plenty of good resources on the life and teachings of Jesus Christ. Look for material published by the Navigators or Scripture Press—clearly outlined workbooks that require *lots* of written responses by the student that apply the teaching to daily life.

Next make membership mean something to those who join; otherwise, why should they bother? Require from everyone the willingness to accept admonition and correction by fellow members, particularly the leaders. Here's the relevant paragraph from one church's constitution:

According to Matthew 18:15–17 the church has the right and duty to expel members whose conduct contradicts their profession, and who transgress any of the divine laws and refuse to be led to heartfelt and open sorrow and repentance, and to the determination of real betterment by the admonitions given them, but continue in sin. For the depriving of membership a two-thirds majority of all votes cast is necessary at a meeting called for that purpose.[12]

Another section on the duties and privileges of members in this constitution requires members to submit any possible lawsuit against fellow members to the church board before bringing it before the civil authorities. (The biblical basis for this rule is found in 1 Cor. 6:1–8.) These sections are gone over carefully with all prospective members so that they know what the church is vigilant to enforce.

Third, establish a clear congregational policy for disciplining with designated responsibilities. In our church we have two main boards, the deacons (including our two pastors) and the trustees. Our members know that if there is behavioral trouble among them, which they have tried and failed to resolve by themselves, then the deacons and pastors will get involved—no one else. In fact the most difficult yet gratifying work in my ministry at Emmaus has been the development of a teamwork approach to crisis intervention. Generally a pastor and a deacon will be the primary contacts in a problem; however the alternatives that this pair offers to the troubled person(s) are those that have already been hammered out in discussion with the entire deacon board. Time-consuming? You bet. But it enables the counselors to speak with authority, so it's worth it.

Helpful Hints

Now that you know the process of discipline, here are twelve tips on discipline from churches which have learned the hard way, as reported to Gordon Schroeder:

A Dozen Tips on Discipline
1. Make your attitude one of encouragement and restoration rather than confrontation and warning.

2. Heed the warning signals of the sin before it grows and act promptly.
3. Make your contact with the errant member personally and immediately.
4. Design a clear plan of restoration to fellowship for them and tell them of it.
5. Put in staff contracts that immoral behavior will result in termination.
6. Be willing to confront the problem even if it puts your job in danger.
7. Involve the leadership in charting the course of counseling, yet use only those counselors who can truly help.
8. If errant persons are avoiding you, try calling on them unannounced.
9. Seek professional help for the person if it is needed. Keep a resource list.
10. Be aware of people who have conquered similar sins and are qualified to help.
11. Avoid delaying the stages of discipline beyond six months for each stage. Delay is the deadliest form of denial.
12. Begin counseling with the person before it becomes a matter for the entire board of leaders. That may suffice.[13]

Toughlove in the Pastoral Search Process

Some dysfunctional congregations will resist the establishment of consistent, biblical discipline. Pastors may wish to admonish or avoid them when candidating. They need to ask search committees, "When have you last used biblical discipline, and what was the result?" Granted, no church should be without a pastor, even if they have problems. Yet pastors can still employ some leverage in helping them to be more accountable. One survey respondent takes an even tougher stance:

> I do not believe that the Lord will send one of His preachers to pastor a Church which has tossed out one who was in obedience to His Word. Ministers ought to [follow] the ethical standards of Physicians and Attorneys who would not take a case wherein one of their comrades was mistreated.

On the other hand, search committees must work harder to examine the background of their candidates, and pastors ought to cooperate fully with them. Perhaps the search committee should deny an interview until the prospective new pastor can supply some references who were *opposed* to him. (Though Emmaus Church didn't require it, I gave them references of some who were opposed to me. It must not have hurt since they hired me!)

Conclusion

The Protestant church scene today resembles the game of musical chairs I used to play in kindergarten, with people marching around chairs in a circle, having one person too many for all the chairs, and scrambling madly for a position when the music stopped. In the same way pastors leap from one church to another, committing the same sins, while their members stay put, repeating their own pet sins with a different pastoral staff member. It's a wearying, demoralizing, frustrating, and foolish game of musical pulpits. Yet we have come to accept and even to justify such a waste of money, time, and people's lives.

Meanwhile, contentious persons (whether clergy or laity) have become far too politically conscious, abusing their power within the local congregation to lord it over fellow members or pastors. Hence nothing less than a spiritual revolution will reinstate the local church as a center for the spiritual discipline and training of committed Christians.

The facts show that it is to the advantage both of the pastor and the local congregation to establish biblical discipline. Both will benefit from longer, more stable pastorates, as well as fewer disruptive influences within the local church. Denominational officials will benefit from more mature congregations which can handle their own conflicts in a redemptive way. Our nation will benefit from seeing the church restored to its primary functions of saving and nurturing the souls of human beings. Above all God will be glorified in his people once again.

Making It Work

In closing, consider two success stories concerning discipline. In one church a member had become critical of the elder board and pastor because a missionary relative of his had been removed from the list of those receiving financial support due to a change in the missionary's beliefs. The leaders of the local congregation went to this man—without the pastor's knowledge—and confronted him according to the procedure of Matthew 18. The man repented. Thus his witness as a godly man in the community was maintained due to the loving confrontation of fellow Christians.

The second story comes from another church. Two brothers had a dispute regarding the settlement of their father's will. Property disposition and cash equalization were plainly stated; however, years of animosity prevented them from having the mutual trust necessary for a settlement. Tension built up throughout the family and fears of legal action mounted.

Then the leaders stepped in, beginning a long process of spiritual counsel, urging each brother to confess and to repent of particular sins committed against the other. To prevent conflict from recurring, the board appointed two persons to oversee the next few steps of negotiating a settlement regarding the will. With the counsel of the whole board, the two appointed persons proposed compromise solutions and kept in direct contact with each brother to correct misunderstandings and allay suspicions. The entire effort was bathed in prayer by the board members and the families involved. After nearly six months of meetings, the brothers reached an agreement regarding the will and now can look ahead to working together in a cooperative, rather than mutually destructive way.

In many undisciplined congregations, such conflicts could lead to widespread conflagration, scapegoating of the pastor, and ultimately a forced exit. Neither of these cases had such repercussions due to the clear expectations that their churches maintain for Christians, obedience to spiritual authority being one of them.

Lay leader, if you do not yet have such a church, help create one. Pastor, if you are not yet serving such a church, find one or work with godly leaders in your own church to make it one. Your members, over time, will conform to their leaders' expectations. Don't sit back and gripe; set the pace.

Keeping each other from sin is difficult work—and worth every minute of it! If we love Jesus Christ enough to protect his name, and love each other enough to guard our reputations as Christians, then we have no choice but to exercise gentle, firm, consistent, prayerful discipline at the local church level. Let us cry out to God in repentance for our compromise with evil! And then let us demonstrate by a compassionate toughness that we will tolerate no more cheap grace which abandons the brother to his sin—and no more musical pulpits!

Appendix A

Questionnaire on Forced Pastoral Exits

General Instructions: This survey concerns church discipline as it relates to forced pastoral exits. If you have been either fired or forced to resign a pastoral post, then you have experienced a forced exit. Even if you have not, please complete the first two pages. All information you provide is extremely important. Write in additional comments whenever you wish. If you have served or are serving more than one church at a time, include only the *largest* church of each multichurch pastorate in your answers. This survey is confidential; I will never divulge your identity to anyone else. You will receive a summary of results for your cooperation. Thank you!

Section A. Basic Information

1. What is your age? ___47___ (average)
2. What is your sex? M __97%__ F __3%__
3. Years in pastorate: __19__ (average)

4. Your denomination or association of independent churches: (47 different denominations or independent churches).

5. Level of training for pastoral work completed:

None	College	Master's	Doctorate
2%	27%	62%	10%

Section B. Church Discipline

"Church discipline" as used here means the process of confronting a sinning Christian with intent to aid confession of the sin and restoration to fellowship: "If your brother sins against you, go and show him his fault, just between the two of you. If he listens to you, you have won your brother over. But if he will not listen, take one or two others along, so that 'every matter may be established by the testimony of two or three witnesses.' If he refuses to listen to them, tell it to the church; and if he refuses to listen even to the church, treat him as you would a pagan or a tax collector" (Matt. 18:15–17).

1. Have you consciously followed this procedure in your ministry?

Yes	No	Not Sure
67%	21%	12%

2. Have you made yourself accountable to a fellow Christian as a form of spiritual discipline?

Yes	No	Not Sure
67%	25%	8%

In recent years, there have been cases where a church member has sued a church for invasion of privacy because he or she was the object of church discipline. Experts say that to avoid losing a lawsuit, a disciplining church must:

    A. State its disciplinary procedure in its bylaws.

    B. Explain its discipline to all prospective members.

    C. Practice discipline consistently and impartially.

3. Of the churches you have pastored, including the present, how many have practiced all of the items A, B, and C as listed above?

    __1__ (average)

4. Give the total number of churches you have pastored:

    __4__ (average)

Section C. Your Career in Ministry

1. Please list your last five pastorates, starting with your current position, and provide the requested information. (Circle either "Yes" or "No" on the indicated questions.)

Church #	Years Served	Were (Or Are) You Forced to Leave?*	Was Your Predecessor Forced to Leave?
1 (current)	_____	Yes No	Yes No
2	Pastors served an	Yes No	Yes No
3	average of 5.7 years in	Yes No	Yes No
4	each church	Yes No	Yes No
5		Yes No	Yes No

*(25% had at least one Yes)

2. Were any of these interim pastorates? (Identify them by number; that is, "#2, #3"): *Yes (10%); No (90%).*

Note: If you did not have any forced departures recorded
    above, you have now finished the questionnaire;
    otherwise, continue.

   3. In each forced exit, what reason did your lay
      leadership give for your departure? (Again,
      please identify churches by number; such as,
      #5—misuse of funds.) (See Chapter 6 for the rea-
      sons behind forced exits.)

Section D. Factors of Forced Pastoral Exits

Complete this section if you were forced to leave one
or more congregations. First, carefully reflect on the
forced exit(s) you have experienced. Then, beside each of
the following statements indicate whether the factors
listed apply to *any* of the forced exits you have endured.
Circle the number that best indicates whether you
strongly agree (SA), agree (A), are neutral (N), disagree
(D), strongly disagree (SD), or don't know (DK) that they
were involved in one or more of your forced exits.
"Strongly agree" (SA) means you are certain that the item
was a factor in your exit; "strongly disagree" (SD) means
you are certain that the item was not a factor in your
exit; "neutral" (N) means you are uncertain about its
being a factor; "don't know" (DK) means that you have
no evidence whatever to form an intelligent opinion.

1. Congregational Factors

The following were significant factors in my forced exit(s): (NOTE: All Percentages from the Group of 95 Forced-Out Pastors.)

	SA	A	N	D	SD	DK
			Percentages			
Unresolved church trauma:	33	28	15	4	14	7
Unrealistic expectations for pastoral performance:	21	35	17	11	14	2
Powerful individuals "lording it over" church leaders:	58	22	5	5	9	1
Lack of people's commitment to follow Christ in life:	22	26	21	12	18	2
Competing power groups within the congregation:	39	31	14	8	6	1
Lack of discipline of contentious members:	33	29	15	8	14	1
Lingering loyalty to previous pastor:	13	21	13	13	36	4
Split over doctrinal issue:	11	14	18	12	39	6
Conflict over new program:	11	21	22	12	30	5
Conflict within pastoral team	22	10	11	13	35	10
Conflict over finances or church expenses /salaries:	10	21	14	11	39	5
Perception that pastor's age or tenure is excessive:	6	6	22	11	18	7

Other (describe: _____

	SA	A	N	D	SD	DK
Only 23 pastors responded:	65	13	9	0	4	9

2. Personal Factors

The following factors were significant factors in my forced exit(s):

	SA	A	N	D	SD	DK
			Percentages			
Sexual sin on my part:	2	2	4	6	82	4
My abuse of alcohol or drugs:	0	1	2	2	91	4
My misuse of church funds:	0	0	2	4	92	2
Divorce or separation from my spouse (whether initiated by me or not):	5	1	2	2	86	4
A "hidden agenda" I brought and tried to force on people:	2	2	10	11	70	5
Being too passive or timid in leadership:	3	22	21	12	40	2
Too domineering in leadership:	2	8	17	19	50	4
Showing favoritism:	0	0	7	17	69	7
Overinvolvement outside the local church:	0	6	8	12	68	6
Significant change in beliefs:	1	2	7	11	75	4
Unrealistic demands I made on the members of my church:	5	6	5	8	73	4
Personal uncertainty of my "call" to be a minister:	1	1	4	4	86	5
Other (describe: _____						
Only 18 pastors responded:	42	21	5	0	26	5

Feel free to write in any additional comments. Return in the envelope provided. Thank you!

Appendix B:

Lay Leader Interview

Name: _____

Address: _____

Phone:_____

INTRODUCTION: This interview concerns the impact of forced pastoral exits on congregations and lay leaders. It consists of eight questions and will take 10–20 minutes to complete. If you are quoted, you will be identified only by denominational affiliation. Please think back to the *one* most traumatic forced pastoral exit your church had and answer the following questions. Use the other side if necessary. Thank you!

1. How did the pastor disappoint your church? (Limit your reasons to no more than two or three please.)
2. How long had he served? How long had his predecessor served?

3. What was your role in the conflict? (For example, were you a mediator, instigator, spectator, or what?)
4. Did the church attempt to apply biblical modes of conflict resolution and discipline? In what way, and what were the results?
5. Was the discipline/conflict resolution process misused in any way? How, and by whom?
6. What difficulties did you and your church experience in all of this? Have the problems persisted?
7. How were your personal relationships affected by this forced exit—with family, friends, fellow members?
8. What counsel would you offer other lay leaders to prevent or to better handle conflicts like these?

Notes

Preface

1. Clifford Tharp, "A Study of the Forced Termination of Southern Baptist Ministers," Nashville: Research Services Department of the Sunday School Board, Southern Baptist Convention (June, 1984), 19.

2. Rodney Crowell, "Spiritual Survival for a Forced Exit," *Leadership*, vol. X, no. 1 (Winter, 1989), 27–30.

Chapter 1: Introduction to the Issue of Forced Exits

1. Menno H. Epp, *The Pastor's Exit* (Winnipeg: CMBC Publications, 1984), 39.

2. U.S. Department of Commerce, Bureau of the Census, *Statistical Abstract of the United States,* 110th ed. (Washington, D.C.: 1990), Table No. 647, "Occupational Tenure, By Occupation: 1987," 393.

3. Speed Leas, "A Study of Involuntary Terminations in Some Presbyterian, Episcopal, and United Church of Christ Congregations," (Washington, D.C.: Alban Institute, 1980), 4.

4. Charles Colson, *Who Speaks For God?* (Westchester, Ill.: Crossway, 1985), 71.

5. Leas, "Involuntary Terminations," 34.

6. Edgar W. Mills, *Career Change Among Ministers* (Ph.D. diss., Harvard University, 1966), 155.

Chapter 2: A Brief History of the Problem

1. H. G. Duncan, "Reactions of Ex-Ministers Toward the Ministry," *Journal of Religion*, XII, 1 (Jan., 1932), 108–9.

2. For the most comprehensive bibliography of this time period, see Mills, *Career Change Among Ministers* (Ph.D. diss., Harvard University, 1966), 163, 167–73.

3. Ibid., 161.

4. Ibid., 67–68.

5. Gerald Jud, Edgar Mills, and Genevieve Burch, *Ex-Pastors: Why Men Leave the Parish Ministry* (Philadelphia: Pilgrim Press, 1970), 51.

6. Harold Myra, "Trauma and Betrayal: Experiences of *Leadership* Readers," *Leadership,* vol. II, no. 1 (Winter, 1981), 44.

7. Charles Rassieur, *Stress Management for Ministers* (Philadelphia: Westminster Press, 1982).

8. Tommy D. Bledsoe, *Case Studies of Georgia Baptist Ministerial Families Who Have Resigned Pastorates Without Immediate Prospects for Another Pastorate* (Ph.D., Georgia State University, 1980), 137–42.

9. Leas, "Involuntary Terminations," 4–5.

10. Ibid., 3–4, 7–8, 10–14, 27, 33, 37, 38.

11. Epp, *The Pastor's Exit,* 28–43.

12. Tharp, "Forced Terminations," 2.

13. Ernest O. White, "Church Minister Termination in the Missouri Baptist Convention—Final Report," (Louisville: Dehoney Center for Study of the Local Church, October, 1989), 8–9.

14. Brooks Faulkner, *Forced Termination* (Nashville: Broadman, 1986).

15. Ibid., 16–28.

16. Richard Schachet, *Rabbis Who Have Left the Pulpit: An Exploration of Attitudes and Alternatives,* (D.Min. diss., Princeton Theological Seminary, 1984), 54.

17. Leslie R. Freedman, "Role-Related Stress in the Rabbinate: A Report on a Nationwide Study of Conservative and Reform Rabbis," *Journal of Reform Judaism,* vol. 32, no. 1 (Winter, 1985), 4–6.

18. Ibid., 3.

Chapter 3: Warning Signals

1. Howard V. Pendley III, "Forced Termination?" *Search* (Fall, 1986), 19–24.

2. Brooks Faulkner, "A Redemptive Approach to Forced Terminations," *Church Administration* (July, 1984), 21.

3. Information on the Retraining Seminar may be obtained from the Career Guidance Section, Church Administration Department, Sunday School Board, Southern Baptist Convention, 127 Ninth Avenue N., Nashville, TN 37234. An outline for a weekend session may be found in Faulkner's book, *Forced Termination* (Nashville: Broadman, 1986), 47–54.

Chapter 4: The Emotional Toll of Forced Exits

1. Russell Cawthon, Jr., "When They Requested He Resign, He Lost More Than a Job," *Church Administration* (July, 1984), 9–11.

2. Leas, "Involuntary Terminations," 21. The percentage is hand-calculated from his data.

3. Ira Survivor, "'You Should Resign,' They Said," *SBC Today* (May, 1984), 15.

Chapter 5: Survival Steps for Pastors and Churches

1. Robert D. Dale, "How to Help a Fellow Minister Who's Been Fired," *Church Administration* (November, 1982), 28.

2. Epp, *The Pastor's Exit,* 49.

Chapter 6: Why Do Forced Exits Happen?

1. Warren Wiersbe, *The Bible Exposition Commentary* (Wheaton, Ill.: Victor, 1989), 2:158.

Chapter 7: How Bad Is It?

1. For those trained in empirical research, I offer the following information: an independent t-test showed the difference between the two subgroup means to be statistically significant at .0339 for a one-tailed test, well within the .05 confidence level set prior to the survey. The t-test value is 1.83233, or .18733 above the critical value of 1.645 necessary for proof at 366 degrees of freedom.

2. I wrote to the American Baptist Convention, the Christian and Missionary Alliance, the Church of God (Anderson), the Christian Church (Disciples of Christ), the Church of the Nazarene, the Evangelical Lutheran Church of America, the Episcopal Church, the General Association of General Baptists, the Lutheran Church Missouri Synod, the Presbyterian Church (PCUSA), the Southern Baptist Convention, and the United Methodist Church. Two made no reply.

3. Leland Duncan. Note to author, November 19, 1990.

4. Robert F. Kohler. Letter to author, May 31, 1991.

5. Faulkner, *Forced Termination,* 14–15.

6. Jackson Carroll and Robert Wilson, *Too Many Pastors? The Clergy Job Market* (New York: Pilgrim Press, 1980), 69.

Chapter 8: The Trouble with Conflict Management

1. Norman Shawchuck, *How to Manage Conflict in the Church: Understanding and Managing Conflict* (Irvine, Calif.: Spiritual Growth Resources, 1983), 35.

2. Ibid., 36.

3. Morton Deutsch, *The Resolution of Conflict* (New Haven: Yale University Press, 1973), 12–15.

4. Ibid., 359–65.

5. Shawchuck, *How to Manage Conflict in the Church*, 46–47.

6. I take as my measure for this claim the difference between the 36 percent of churches in my survey which have forced out two successive pastors, and the figure of 23 percent reported by Speed Leas in 1980.

7. G. Douglass Lewis, *Resolving Church Conflicts: A Case Study Approach for Local Congregations* (New York: Harper & Row, 1981), 32.

Chapter 9: Toughlove Applied to Churches and Pastors

1. J. Carl Laney, *A Guide to Church Discipline* (Minneapolis: Bethany, 1985), 47.

2. John Howard Yoder, "Binding and Loosing" *Concern #14* (February, 1967), 23.

3. John MacArthur, *Shepherdology* (Panorama City, Calif.: The Master's Fellowship, 1989), 224.

4. Alexander Strauch, *Biblical Eldership* (Littleton, Colo.: Lewis & Roth, 1988), 106.

5. Lynn Buzzard and Thomas Brandon, Jr., *Church Discipline and the Courts* (Wheaton: Tyndale, 1987), 267.

6. Marlin Jeschke, *Discipling in the Church* (Scottdale, Penn.: Herald Press, 1988), 88.

7. MacArthur, *Shepherdology,* 224; Jack Wyrtzen, "Restoration: Fellowship or Leadership?" *Word of Life Fellowship 1989 Annual,* 27.

8. J. Carl Laney, *A Guide to Church Discipline,* 167.

9. Gordon F. Schroeder, *An Analysis of the Current Practice of Church Discipline Among Churches Pastored by Graduates of Dallas Theological Seminary* (D.Min. diss., Dallas Theological Seminary, 1986), 23.

10. Ibid., 59–60.

11. Jeschke, *Discipling,* 112–16.

12. *Constitution of the Emmaus Mennonite Church* (Revised September, 1990), 4.

13. Schroeder, *Analysis,* 112–24.

Annotated Bibliography

Church Discipline and Leadership
Books

Adams, Jay E. *Handbook of Church Discipline.* Grand Rapids: Zondervan, 1986. This is a very comprehensive, practical, and biblically based resource.

Buzzard, Lynn R. and Thomas S. Brandon, Jr., *Church Discipline and the Courts.* Wheaton: Tyndale, 1986. Two Christian Legal Society experts review churches' legal liabilities and defenses against lawsuits. They include an extensive treatment of the Guinn case.

Jeschke, Marlin. *Discipling in the Church.* Scottdale, Penn.: Herald Press, 1988. Jeschke provides a mature and reasonable defense of discipline with a balanced treatment of excommunication and avoidance.

Laney, J. Carl. *A Guide to Church Discipline.* Minneapolis: Bethany, 1985. Laney's book may be the best written on discipline. It contains a helpful flow chart on procedure, plus results from his own survey.

Strauch, Alexander. *Biblical Eldership: An Urgent Call to Restore Biblical Church Leadership.* Littleton, Colo.: Lewis & Roth, 1988. Strauch makes a systematic study of major biblical texts on elders and deacons with a strong defense of elder rule in the local congregation.

Articles and Studies

Yoder, John H. "Binding and Loosing," *Concern* 14 (1967): 2–32. This essay is a Mennonite theologian's treatment of Matthew 18:15–17, which contains good replies to misconceptions of church discipline and excuses for not using it.

Forced Pastoral Exits
Books

Epp, Menno H. *The Pastor's Exit: The Dynamics of Involuntary Termination.* Winnipeg: CMBC Publishing, 1984. This book contains case studies of thirty-five forcibly terminated Canadian Mennonite pastors. The author aptly describes congregational attitudes and responses to involuntary termination.

Faulkner, Brooks. *Forced Termination.* Nashville: Broadman Press, 1986. Faulkner is a Southern Baptist career-guidance counselor who suggests retraining of pastors and church boards as an alternative to firing.

Leas, Speed. *Should the Pastor Be Fired? How to Deal Constructively with Clergy-Lay Conflict.* Washington, D.C.: Alban Institute, 1980. This study contains insightful sections on warning signals of, and survival steps for forced exits; yet it lacks Bible-based criteria for when not to force out a pastor.

Articles and Studies

Cawthon, Russell C., Jr. "When They Requested He Resign, He Lost More Than His Job," *Church*

Administration (July, 1984): 9–11. This is possibly the best summary of forced-exit stresses in print, yet it lacks concrete suggestions for reducing or managing them.

Crowell, Rodney J. "Spiritual Survival for a Forced Exit," *Leadership,* vol. X, no. 1 (Winter, 1989): 26–30. This is one pastor's account of a mismatch and subsequent forced exit.

Dale, Robert D. "How to Help a Fellow Minister Who's Been Fired," *Church Administration* (November, 1982): 28–30. Dale offers wise counsel on helping suffering pastors to survive, heal, and grow through a forced exit while preparing for the future.

Leas, Speed B. "A Study of Involuntary Terminations in Some Presbyterian, Episcopal, and United Church of Christ Congregations," 41 pp. Washington, D.C.: The Alban Institute, 1980. This is a landmark work filled with usable data on forced exit factors and stresses.

(Name Withheld). "When You're Forced Out," *Leadership,* vol. XII, no. 2 (Spring, 1991): 106–10. A fired pastor discovers he needed to return to ministry to overcome his fear of failure and implement what he learned from his termination.

Pendley, Howard V. III. "Forced Termination?" *Search* (Fall, 1986): 19–24. Pendley shows pastors how to stand their ground against pleas to resign.

Price, Roy C. "When the Pastor Gets Fired," *Leadership,* vol. IV, no. 4 (Fall, 1983): 50–55. Price offers solidly scriptural reasons on when to fire or not fire the pastor, adding good suggestions on how to cope with a forced exit.

Tharp, J. Clifford, Jr. "A Study of the Forced Termination of Southern Baptist Ministers," 48 pp. Nashville: Research Services Department of the

Sunday School Board, June, 1984. This is the largest survey analysis to date on forced exits. It emphasizes the candidating pastor's need to know a church's termination history.

White, Ernest O. "Church Minister Termination in the Missouri Baptist Convention," 39 pp. Louisville: The Dehoney Center, Southern Baptist Theological Seminary, October, 1989. White compares forced-exit rates in various state Conventions of Southern Baptists.

Ex-Pastors
Books

Jud, Gerald J. and others. *Ex-Pastors: Why Men Leave the Parish Ministry.* Philadelphia: United Church Press, 1970. This study of 241 ex-pastors in the United Church of Christ found that many pastors were unhappy with the church's lack of relevance to modernity.

Mills, Edgar Wendell, Jr. *Leaving the Pastorate: A Study in the Social Psychology of Career Change.* Ph.D. dissertation, Harvard University, 1966. Mills' survey of sixty Presbyterian ex-pastors anticipates many of the conflicts that surfaced in later studies.

Schachet, Richard I. *Rabbis Who Have Left the Pulpit: An Exploration of Attitudes and Alternatives.* D.Min. dissertation, Princeton Theological Seminary, 1984. The author reflects on a weekend summit with six ex-rabbis now in "tentmaking" ministries.

Articles and Studies

Duncan, H. G. "Reactions of Ex-Ministers Toward the Ministry," *Journal of Religion* 12 (January, 1932): 100–115. This early study of 111 ex-pastors found that the best-trained men, not the worst, were with-drawing from pastoral ministry in disillusionment.

Nauss, Allen. "Lessons From the Lives of Our Graduates: A Follow-Up of Graduates Not in the Active LC-MS Ministry," 31 pp. Springfield, Mo., 1973. This study of eighty-six Lutheran Missouri Synod ex-pastors revealed that conflicts in their first six years of ministry strongly influenced their decisions to leave.

Wickman, Charles A. "Ex-Pastors: Why Did They Leave?" *Christianity Today,* (January 21, 1983): 41. Wickman's informal survey of twenty-six ex-pastors suggests that most left due to the lack of time the pastoral ministry gives for family life.

Stress in the Pastorate
Books

Beasley-Murray, Paul. *Pastors Under Pressure.* Eastbourne, England: Kingsway Publications, 1989. This is a succinct analysis of why many United Kingdom pastors are leaving their posts. The author includes pointed recommendations.

Bratcher, Edward B. *The Walk-on-Water Syndrome.* Waco, Tex.: Word, 1984. A seasoned veteran of ministry warns against unrealistic expectations and spiritual immaturity on the part of clergy and laity alike.

Carroll, Jackson W. and Robert Wilson. *Too Many Pastors? The Clergy Job Market.* New York: Pilgrim, 1980. Two researchers share results from their twelve-denomination study of clergy oversupply and its consequences.

Shelley, Marshall. *Well-Intentioned Dragons.* Waco, Tex.: Word, 1985. "When attacked by a dragon, do not become one" is Marshall's wise counsel on dealing with problem people in the congregation.

Smith, Donald P. *Clergy in the Crossfire: Coping with
Role Conflicts in the Ministry.* Philadelphia: Westminster, 1973. Smith pinpoints the role conflicts
inherent in ministry, suggesting how to establish
clear goals and feedback. No mention of discipline.

Articles and Studies

Freedman, Leslie R. "Role-Related Stress in the Rabbinate: A Report on a Nationwide Study of Conservative and Reform Rabbis," *Journal of Reform
Judaism,* vol. 32, no. 1 (Winter, 1985): 1–7. One in
four of 1,342 rabbis surveyed called their job "very
stressful." Freedman, a psychologist, recommends
psychotherapy. Consider the source.

Conflict Management

Shawchuck, Norman. *How to Manage Conflict in the
Church.* Irvine, Calif.: Spiritual Growth Resources,
1983. This workbook helps you discern your primary and back-up conflict management styles.

Studies in Related Fields

O'Toole, Patricia. *Corporate Messiah: The Hiring and
Firing of Million-Dollar Managers.* New York:
William Morrow and Company, 1984. O'Toole's
case studies show that huge contracts used to lure
corporate messiahs bring unrealistically high
expectations which often lead to their dethrone-
ment. Pastors experience the same pitfalls without
the perks.

Sonnenfeld, Jeffrey. *The Hero's Farewell: What Happens When CEO's Retire.* New York: Oxford Press,
1988. The author examines the various "departure
styles" of corporate leaders, which is very applica-
ble to pastoral predecessors.